Growing Up Straight:
What Families Should Know
About Homosexuality

by
George Alan Rekers

MOODY PRESS

CHICAGO

All Scripture quotations in this book are from the *New American Standard Bible*, © 1960, 1962, 1963, 1968, 1971, 1972, 1973, 1975, and 1977 by The Lockman Foundation, and are used by permission.

Library of Congress Cataloging in Publication Data

Rekers, George Alan.
  Growing up straight.

  Bibliography: p. 145
  Includes index.
  1. Homosexuality and Christianity. I. Title.
BR115.H6R45 1982   261.8'35766   82-8197
ISBN 0-8024-0156-2

Printed in the United States of America

For the hundreds of children, teenagers, and parents who have allowed me to serve them in the collaborative effort to find delivery from homosexuality and to work toward the fulfillment of normal marriage and family life.

CONTENTS

Preface

This book is based on my professional experience as a clinical psychologist and on understanding gleaned from being a father, husband, and foster parent. Thus I am indebted to many more people than I can cite in this short space. At the risk of omitting many, I wish to mention a few who played significant roles in the development of my research and of this book.

In June 1970, a year after the infamous "Stonewall Riot" that marked the start of the gay liberation movement, my major professor at the University of California at Los Angeles, Dr. O. Ivar Lovaas, assigned me a clinical research project on childhood sexual identity disorders. The project subsequently grew into my Ph.D. dissertation in psychology. Because of his expertise in child psychology, Dr. Lovaas launched my career in the area of childhood sexual identity problems as no other mentor could. I am grateful also to the National Science Foundation for my graduate fellowship at UCLA, which supported my doctoral study.

When I was a visiting scholar at the Center for the Behavioral Sciences at Harvard University, the Foundations' Fund for Research in Psychiatry provided me a grant to extend my research in this area. Then, for the past eight years, the National Institute of Mental Health has provided me over half a million dollars to conduct research on the early identification and treatment of childhood gender problems, with a view to preventing homosexuality, transsexualism, and transvestism. I gratefully acknowledge those sources of funding.

I also owe gratitude to Ed Welge, Bill Rehwald, Judd Swihart, Dean Wood, Horace Brelsford, and Bob Buckler, past and present members of the board of directors of the Logos Research Institute, Inc., which has sponsored my research for many years; they supported me as president of the Institute in ways too numerous to mention, and made my long-term research project possible.

While living in Florida, I was fortunate to have the friendship and support of my pastor, Mike Braun, of the Community Evangelical Free Church of Gainesville, who helped me through some difficult conflicts with the gay liberation activists in town. Mike Braun and I coauthored another book, *The Christian in an Age of Sexual Eclipse* (Wheaton, Ill.: Tyndale, 1981), which helped inspire the present book to parents. Mike also gave me insightful editorial comment on an earlier draft of this book and directly contributed to this volume in chapter 9.

My friend Reed Bell, M.D., Chief of Pediatrics at Sacred Heart Hospital in Pensacola, Florida, did more than anyone else to encourage me to see this book to its completion. I appreciate, too, all the editorial work provided by Moody Press, especially the attention devoted to this manuscript by Beverly J. Burch, former Administrative Editor.

My wife, Sharon, and our three sons, Steven, Andrew, and Matthew, have tolerated Daddy's book manuscript all over the dining room table in various stages of writing and editing. I was able to write this book only with their permission, cooperation, and love.

I have devoted a dozen years of professional life to clinical work and research on preventing sexual abnormalities in order to promote a future of normal family fulfillment for today's children and teenagers. I hope my professional work and this book will help many others experience the same wonderful blessing of family life that I have experienced. This book was written for all those who want to make sure every child has the opportunity to grow up straight.

Introduction

Several years ago, as an undergraduate, I was a leader in the college department of our small Baptist church in Southern California. One evening, while I was leading a time of singing and sharing, a young stranger walked into the home where we had gathered and sat quietly observing us. He was well dressed and good looking. He seemed interested in our fellowship and in our testimonies of God's guidance in our lives. Yet all the while he seemed discouraged and sad.

Hoping to have an opportunity to talk to him about Christ, I made a beeline for him as our meeting broke up. At the same time he made a similar run for the door and his parked car. I plotted my trajectory with the precision of one skilled in the baptistic art of bodily ballistics. Our paths intersected just in front of the grill of his waiting get-away car. It was a direct hit! But it was the only success that I would have that night.

We—or better, I—began to talk. Hi! Glad he came. How did he like the sharing? Who brought him? What did he think of what we talked about? And, eventually, had he ever made a commitment to Jesus Christ similar to the ones that he heard about tonight?

Yes, he was glad he came, too. He found the sharing "interesting." But his answer to my question about his relationship with Christ completely took the wind out of my sails. With an air of deep sadness he said, "You see, I could never be a Christian; I am a homosexual. My psychiatrist told me I should stop repressing my sexual feelings and try to adjust to life in the homosexual world."

I had never talked with an admitted homosexual before, and, frankly, I was speechless. We didn't say anything for a moment. Then I said something like, "I wish I could help," and he said something like, "Thank you." Then we said good-bye.

The incident disturbed me deeply. A few days later I talked to an older Christian brother whom I respected deeply. He said with all seriousness, "I think the only thing you can do for homosexuals is let them adjust to being a homosexual or shoot them."

"Let them adjust, or shoot them." Few things bother me more than an idea as fundamentally opposed to the gospel of Jesus Christ as that one. If anything is a lie, it is that there are some people and some problems in life that are beyond the redemptive power of the gospel of Jesus Christ.

Somehow the worldly view of sexual determinism has crept into the church. It is surprising how many Christians see homosexuality as irreversible. Tragically, rampant homophobia—fear of homosexuality—inhibits a ministry to a large group of suffering people. They are suffering not because of social intolerance but because sin is ravaging their lives. Christians should have something to say about breaking the power of sin in life.

Yet so often Christians do not say anything about the gospel's power to restore the sexual life because they

14

have been deceived by the big lie that behavior is set; that men are programmed; that you are what you are, and there is never any helping it.

In addition, we have been told that anyone who "imposes" standards of self-control on sexual impulses is "naive" or "repressive" or both, and we have believed it. Consequently we agonize over the "conjugal rights" of prison inmates, and we worry about astronauts deprived of sexual activity on long interplanetary junkets. To be sexually unfulfilled is becoming a tragedy ranking not far behind being denied "life, liberty, and the pursuit of happiness."

I am not sure just who is being naive here—the person who believes in the possibility of self-control in one's sex life, or the one who devoutly holds to the impossibility of self-control. Sexual determinism is the big lie of the world. The world wishes to believe that sexual expression is ultimately undeniable and that there is no use in resisting various sexual impulses.

As a rule, Christians have successfully resisted such rationalization for permissiveness regarding heterosexual activity. That has not been the case, however, with the average Christian's view of homosexuality. Many evangelical Christians hold a very worldly, unbiblical view of the problem in denying that it can be solved. No doubt this has arisen partly because of simple homophobia and a wish to shy away from the problem. Nevertheless, much of it stems from acceptance of the lie of sexual determinism.

What is the truth about homosexuality? What is it, and what are its roots? Is it really a problem? Can it be prevented, or is it an inescapable trap? What are the sources of homosexual temptations, and how can they be resisted? How can one triumph over homosexuality?

The answers to those questions form the basis of this book.

15

I
The Truth About Homosexuality

1

What All Parents Need to Know About Homosexuality

"I'm just so worried that I simply *had* to see you, doctor. I really should have come in a long time ago, but I couldn't work up the courage to tell my mom and dad that I wanted to talk to a psychologist. So I just waited until I started college last week before I came in on my own." With his eyes glued to some speck on the carpet, Kirk blurted out those words in his first visit to my office.

After much hesitation, he revealed what had brought him to see me. "You see, I—I'm worried that I might not be exactly normal in my sex life later on. I've never had a steady girl friend. I like girls, but I guess I'm a little shy when it comes to asking a girl for a date. I just get so nervous and tense when there's a girl that I especially like and when I really want to talk to her.

"But that's not all that worries me, I'm afraid. You know, my best friends are guys. In fact, I have a best friend—and, well, it's so easy to be with him, to talk with him, and I really care for him. We're very close friends. There's nothing I wouldn't do for him. And

19

that brings me to my main worry. I really want to get married someday and have kids, but I'm really wondering if there is something wrong with me. Maybe I just wasn't born a heterosexual. Do you know what I mean?"

For the rest of the counseling session, and for the next two sessions, the picture emerged. On two occasions, Kirk had been involved in sexual activity with another teenage boy who had initiated that activity, and in earlier childhood he had been involved in some common types of sex play with boys and girls. He had never excelled in sports at school, he had always been a little shy, and he had difficulty relating socially to girls. But he did not have an exclusive, or even a predominant, sexual interest toward males.

Research on human sexuality indicates that more than a third of all adult men have gone through a phase of sexual interest in other males, even to the point of sexual contact with another male, but only 3 or 4 percent continue a lifelong pattern of homosexuality.[1] Therefore, Kirk should not believe that his earlier sex play with another boy has doomed him to homosexuality for a lifetime.

His fear was what we call "homophobia"—that is, an unrealistic fear of homosexuality, sometimes based on a few episodes of sexual experimentation with the same-sexed partners. Because of past experiences, Kirk mistook his affection for his best friend for homosexuality. As a result, he was seeing less and less of his friend for fear that their relationship might look like homosexuality to others.

WHAT PARENTS NEED TO KNOW ABOUT HOMOPHOBIA AND FRIENDSHIP

Research suggests that empathy and friendship occur most easily between persons of the same sex. Friendship love is both normal and desirable. The Old Testament describes this kind of close friendship between David and Jonathan (1 Samuel 18:14; 20:1-42; 2 Samuel 1:26).

By itself, deep caring for a person of the same sex is no indicator of homosexuality. Parents should not suspect their child is homosexual merely because of a close friendship with someone of the same sex. A completely normal heterosexual can have a very deep and loving relationship with a person of the same sex without being sexually involved. By contrast, the majority of male homosexual acts are actually superficial and devoid of caring, although some homosexual relationships do involve close emotional attachments.

It is very important for parents to teach their children the distinction between close emotional attachments and sexual relationships. Confusion on this point might accidentally contribute to homosexual experimentation by their child.

Christians like Kirk can suffer needless anxiety and self-doubt as a result of a lack of knowledge about true homosexuality. Knowing the difference between homosexuality and friendship can help parents spare their children from unwarranted fear and anxiety over falsely labeled "homosexuality."

Ever since Satan deceived Eve, the devil has used the strategy of mixing a little truth with a healthy dose of error in order to implant fear and confusion. Misunderstanding and the resulting need to rationalize can lead to the bondage of a destructive behavior pattern. Had Kirk not received corrective counseling, he might have given up hope of entering into a normal married life. He might have taken the so-called easy way out and given in to the homosexual advances of a friend. He might have believed the error that he was born homosexual. An informed parent could have spared Kirk this anxiety and fear.

WHAT IS HOMOSEXUALITY?

It is misleading to lump all homosexuals into one group, because there are many different types of homosexuality. Homosexuals differ in the way and the degree to which they are tempted. They differ in the degree to which they are able to respond heterosexually. They differ somewhat in their childhood histories. They also differ with respect to the number of partners that they have had, although by and large, homosexuals are more promiscuous than heterosexuals.

Some homosexual men are effeminate, but others are extremely masculine in appearance and behavior. Some are emotionally repulsed by members of the opposite sex and therefore prefer partners of the same sex in reaction to that repulsion. Others, in contrast, are emotionally indifferent to members of the opposite sex or are equally attracted to members of both sexes.

Because many people are confused about homosexuality, we should carefully define the term *homosexual*. It is a confusing term unless we carefully distinguish between (1) homosexual behavior, (2) homosexual lust, and (3) homosexual temptation.

HOMOSEXUAL BEHAVIOR

Homosexual behavior is the physical contact between two or more persons of the same sex, recognized by each as a sexual contact and usually resulting in physiological sexual arousal. There are many different types of such physical contact, but all are instances of homosexual behavior whether or not sexual climax results.

Every type of homosexual behavior is abnormal, because the normal standard is loving sexual contact between a man and a woman married to each other. Every homosexual act is a substitute for a normal sexual act and therefore competes with normal sexual behavior in the individual. Whether a person engages in homosexual behavior willingly or as a result of homosexual rape or mental disturbance, it is always a perversion of normal human sexual expression. It is my conviction that if homosexual behavior is due to mental disturbance or unwilling victimization, that mental patient or rape victim is not morally accountable. Likewise, I feel that if a young child becomes unwittingly involved in homosexual behavior out of curiosity or because of influence by another individual, he is not morally accountable.

Any homosexual behavior not resulting from victimization or mental disturbance is not only abnormal but also immoral. Such behavior requires a moral choice and often a series of moral choices.

Human beings are not mindless robots programmed to perform one set of sexual actions rather than another. Each human being has the biological capability of sexually interacting with many other persons (or objects). Any sexual behavior requires that a person consciously cooperate with his or her sexual partner to enable his or her body to respond sexually. Because of the voluntary nature of sexual activity, each person bears moral responsibility for his or her sexual behavior.

HOMOSEXUAL LUST

An individual can become homosexually aroused without actual physical contact with a partner. For example, a man might look at a picture of another male and entertain thoughts about having a sexual relationship with the pictured male.

Dwelling on the desire to have another person of the

same sex as a sexual partner is homosexual lust. It may be a purely mental process without actual physiological arousal, or it may result in physical arousal. In some cases, a person may combine homosexual thoughts with masturbation. Homosexual lust therefore includes homosexual desires and thoughts themselves; mental or visual attention to homosexual materials, resulting in physical arousal; or mental or visual attention to homosexual material, combined with masturbation.

All homosexual lust is abnormal and fights against normal sexual adjustment. Each instance of homosexual lust conditions the nervous system to an even stronger responsiveness to homosexual stimulation.

Except in cases of severe mental disturbance, homosexual lust is not only abnormal but also immoral. Jesus made it clear that lust is the moral equivalent of illicit sexual conduct (Matthew 5:28).

HOMOSEXUAL TEMPTATION

Some children are troubled by homosexual temptations. Homosexual temptation is the appeal of a sexual relationship with a member of the same sex. It is the urge or desire to think about, dwell on, or engage in such a relationship. What should parents know about such urges, and what should children be told about them?

Some people are never troubled by the homosexual temptation. The idea is simply not appealing to them, and in fact, may even be repulsive. But other people experience temptations to engage in either homosexual behavior or homosexual lust. The thought of having sexual relations with a member of the same sex is appealing. And when the thought first crosses the mind, temptation has occurred.

A simple temptation to lust or behave homosexually is in itself not immoral; morality applies to what the person does after experiencing the temptation. If a person ignores the temptation and refuses to act upon it in thought or deed, a morally good decision was made. But if a person experiences the homosexual temptation and dwells on the thought, it can become homosexual lust and even lead to homosexual behavior. Yielding to the temptation in thought or in deed is the immoral act. Older children and teenagers usually can learn the difference between temptation, lust, and immoral action.

Although a homosexual temptation is not, by itself, immoral, it is abnormal and undesirable, as is any temptation to become sexually involved with anyone except one's married partner. Children should be taught that all sexual relationships outside of marriage are abnormal and wrong. As they reach later childhood and adolescence, their parents should teach them the difference between sexual temptation, sexual lust, and immoral sexual behavior.

To prevent confusion and distress, parents need to teach their children the difference between homosexuality and friendship, and to warn them about the three kinds of homosexual entrapments. The first, the trap of homosexual temptation, is abnormal but not immoral if the temptation is resisted.

The second is the trap of homosexual lust, which is not only abnormal but also immoral. Lust will undermine the process of normal sexual adjustment necessary for a future of happy marriage and family life. Children must be warned to avoid homosexual lust because it destroys normal development, it is abnormal, and it is sinful.

Homosexual behavior, trap number 3, is the deepest of all. It is destructive to the normal sexual adjustment of both the individual and his partner, it is abnormal, and it is immoral.

Wise parents take a preventive, educative approach

25

to spare their children the agony of learning the hard way about these real and enticing traps, which are often camouflaged in our society.[2]

---

1. A. C. Kinsey, W. B. Pomeroy, and C. E. Martin, *Sexual Behavior in the Human Male* (Philadelphia: Saunders, 1948).
2. See Michael Braun and George A. Rekers, *The Christian in an Age of Sexual Eclipse* (Wheaton, Ill.: Tyndale, 1981).

2

"Gay Liberation"—The Lure of a Deceptive Fantasy World

One or more times every week, it seems, a regular reader of newspapers and magazines will come across an item on homosexuality. Not every item in the news paints the rosy picture that the organizers of "gay liberation" would try to project.

During the week that I began to write this chapter, for example, I read a letter to a newspaper advice columnist from a young college freshman who described his heartache, frustration, guilt, and depression resulting from his homosexual life-style. He yearned for a normal life in the future, and he desperately wanted to get married and have children someday, rather than continue in his empty life-style.

Not long after I had read about this troubled college boy, I came across another nationally syndicated newspaper story about the strange double life of a schoolteacher, which was discovered after he was murdered. His landlord found his naked body in his apartment, which was filled with pictures of nude men. The police investigators concluded that the teacher's secret homosexual life-style most likely led to his murder.

In addition to such regular news stories about the unpleasant lives of homosexual individuals, the papers have carried reports of political action in recent years on the issue of homosexuality. Ordinances have been considered by voters on the issue of whether or not to grant special legal support to homosexuals. Voters in Wichita, Kansas; St. Paul, Minnesota; and Miami, Florida decided in highly publicized referendums against granting legal approval to homosexual lifestyles.

There was a time when homosexuality was not so readily publicized. In fact, only members of the helping professions heard much about cases of homosexuality. Most people suffering from various behavioral disorders, including homosexuality, would consult a clergyman first, and many would seek no other help. Among the secular helping professions, physicians, psychiatrists, and psychologists usually dealt with people concerning homosexual behavior. Until recently, almost all members of those professions considered homosexual behavior an abnormal deviation requiring treatment. People troubled by homosexuality were helped in confidence, with no public fanfare.

As we shall see, a vocal minority within the secular professions has recently argued that homosexual practices should be considered normal variations in a broad spectrum of socially acceptable sexual behavior.[1]

At the same time, homosexuality has been given increasing public attention. It is rather commonplace to read accounts of sexual liberationists who publicly advocate the practice of homosexuality as well as other forms of unmarried sexual expression. On television, in the papers, and in movies, we are increasingly exposed to the arguments of the liberationists. For this reason, parents need to be aware of the gay liberation philosophy in order to teach their children to evaluate it correctly. Do the liberationists really offer greater liberty? Is it possible to promote total sexual freedom with no judgment about what is right, proper, or normal?

"LIBERATION" FROM REALITY

"LIBERATION" FROM BIOLOGICAL REALITY

In their pursuit of so-called freedom, the sexual liberationists seek to obliterate any standards of normality and abnormality.[2] Under the banner of democratic freedoms, they push against the boundaries of biological reality itself. The humanist cannot tolerate any boundary that might restrict his autonomy. He rejects the concept that a Creator fashioned the world with biological, social, and moral boundaries. To admit to such boundaries would be seen as defeat, since the humanist, who sees man as the measure of all things, judges progress in terms of man's overcoming physical and social limitations by technology, education, social planning, or other human efforts.[3]

Parents should point out to children first of all that the basic biology of sexuality logically suggests the norm of heterosexuality. The basic biological make-up of male and female anatomy should suggest the norm of heterosexuality. The survival of the human race (which humanists seem to hold as a basic value) would obviously be threatened by wholesale rejection of heterosexual relations. But the humanist demands liberation from the natural order of the universe.

"LIBERATION" FROM PSYCHOLOGICAL REALITY

The sexual liberationist also pushes against innate psychological boundaries. Motherhood roles are often hastily abandoned.[4] Responsibility and duty for child-rearing are questioned. Marital fidelity is laughed at as an antiquated morality.[5] And yet the resultant suffering

29

of the children, the suffering of the spouse, and the suffering of the liberated give evidence to a real psychological boundary that has been violated. In the past, psychiatry and psychology viewed homosexuality as sexual deviation warranting therapeutic intervention. But humanists have ignored the possibility that this view was based on nature and have worked to change the terminology that psychiatrists use. In this word game, the humanists act as though the mere manipulation of our terminology about the world will change the world itself. Gay liberationists declared all homosexuals "cured" when they succeeded in persuading the American Psychiatric Association to remove homosexuality from the list of mental disorders. They had fought and won the battle of rhetoric.

But did that political action change psychological reality itself? Had the boundary been pushed out of the way? Or had the liberationists only succeeded in renaming the border?

"LIBERATION" FROM MARITAL REALITY

The practical outgrowth of humanism has been the extreme forms of the women's liberation movement and the gay liberation movement. The documents of the radical feminist movement endorse a rejection of heterosexual norms.[6] Radical feminists have written: "Heterosexual relationships are by their very nature oppressive to women in the male dominated society."[7] And "The end of the institution of marriage is a necessary condition for the liberation of women. Therefore, it is important for us to encourage women to leave their husbands and not to live individually with men. We must build alternatives to marriage."[8]

If the heterosexual standard of normality is abandoned, captivity will no longer be recognized for what

30

it is. I once served as an expert witness in a child custody case initiated by a bisexual mother. Her bisexual behavior had destroyed her marriage, and she followed the liberationists' urgings to leave her husband and to fight for the children. In the midst of the custody battle, while fighting for her "rights" to her bisexual life-style, she did not notice that she was captive to a behavior pattern that robbed her children of the opportunity to grow up in their natural home. She did not notice that she was captive to a behavior pattern that had led to a long series of broken relationships.

Ironically, captivity to a homosexual or bisexual life-style is often called "freedom." The normal boundaries for a fulfilling family life are violated under the banner of liberation. This woman succeeded in pushing against the natural boundary of family constraints, but was she really free?

"LIBERATION" FROM SPIRITUAL REALITY

At its roots, the struggle of the humanists is an attempt to remove God and His standards for sexual behavior from the universe. It is the unproved presupposition that God does not exist that provides their launching point.

The healing, the forgiveness, and the power of the gospel are all rejected in favor of self-centered goals.[9] Self becomes the center of the universe, displacing God. Selfish desires become the only guiding force, displacing divine commands.[10] Pursuit of selfish sexuality displaces pursuit of obedience to God's standards for righteousness.[11]

With the individual as the autonomous center of his own ethical decision-making, no humanist wants to be told that his sexual behavior is perverted, abnormal, or deviant. So a new doctrine is born: everyone should be free to do what he wishes. No independent standard defines what is normal and what is abnormal; each case is judged subjectively. Anyone who suggests a universal norm is shouted down as an offender of individual rights.

THE GAY LIBERATION MOVEMENT

In what way is the gay liberation movement a recognizable social movement? What are its goals, objectives, and modes of social activism? Why should parents be aware of its tactics?

Historically in our country, most people who participated in homosexual activity attempted to keep their sexual practices a secret from people in their school, family, or work life. In most social circles, an admission of homosexual practices was unpopular and shameful, and the social stigma encouraged homosexuals to keep their practices a closely guarded secret or even to abandon homosexual behavior altogether. That pattern in the past worked for the welfare of children, who were largely unaware of homosexuality.

Today the issue is often presented as either staying "in the closet" or "coming out." Sadly, a more "tolerant" society may be locking more people into a pattern of destructive behavior rather than liberating them. Many men and women with homosexual behavior have openly admitted their sexual lives and have formed "gay liberation" organizations that vigorously promote the homosexual life-style. That poses a threat for children growing up in our society today.

A CLOSET BY ANY OTHER NAME

Homosexual activists have revolted against society's rejection of their life-style. Leaders of this revolt have defined a "gay" person as a practicing homosexual without any shame, anxiety, guilt, misgivings, or regret over his or her sexual behavior.[12] Gay liberation groups regard homosexual practices as positive, healthy, and desirable behavior to be encouraged in developing youth and to be fully accepted as normal in modern society. The term *gay* has been used by leaders of the homosexual revolt to identify a value system that regards homosexual practices as a legitimate part of an alternative life-style.

Unlike twenty years ago, elementary school children now commonly use the word *gay* to refer to homosexuality. (Parents today might ask themselves, Did I know what a homosexual was when *I* was in elementary school?) It is common to see newspaper articles using such terminology as "National Gay Task Force," "The Gay Switchboard," a "Gay Men's Health Project," the "Gay Teachers Association," and "the Gay Rights National Lobby." What really is meant is "the National Homosexual Task Force," or "The Homosexual Switchboard."

It has been pointed out by experts on English usage that the use of the word *gay* to mean "homosexual" is illegitimate and unfortunate. It is difficult to find a satisfactory synonym for the original meaning of "gay" in normal language. On the other hand, there is no need to develop a new word for "homosexual," since the meaning of that word is well understood.

Perhaps homosexuals have the right to give their perversion any pseudonym they desire, but to paraphrase Shakespeare, "A closet by any other name is a closet all the same."

SEXUAL ANARCHY

Most parents today grew up in a society in which homosexual acts were illegal. But children today are growing up in a different environment. Although many modern nations still enforce laws of varying severity against homosexual practices, some important exceptions are Sweden, England, Canada, the Netherlands, and France, which have no laws against homosexual activity between consenting adult citizens. Most states in the United States have had long-standing laws against homosexual behavior, but Illinois, in 1961, removed its law against homosexual acts, and several other states have similarly removed laws against any sexual practices (including homosexual practices) between consenting adults.

In spite of the exceptions, homosexuals are still a minority within societies that either outlaw or generally oppose homosexual behavior. As a result, they have developed a subculture in which to relate (sometimes secretly) with one another and to cope with the disapproval of the rest of society. This is the context of the modern homosexual revolt.

In the 1950s, prohomosexual activist Henry Hay founded the Mattachine Foundation and its successor, the Mattachine Society. Dorr Legg founded ONE, Inc. The Daughters of Bilitis was founded as an independent lesbian organization in San Francisco around the same time. Shortly after, the Society for Individual Rights was founded as a prohomosexual organization. Those organizations were formed as minority group efforts to revolt against the mainstream of American cultural values.

Henry Hay, founding father of the homosexual revolt movement, was also an active member of the Communist Party in the United States, where he developed skills in generating leadership for an unpopular minority-group movement. Hay and other homosexual revolt leaders took a low-key approach in their early efforts. Those early organizations worked quietly behind the scenes to educate homosexuals and the general public, to counsel homosexuals with legal problems, and to seek changes in sex laws. In general, they discouraged open militancy and preferred to work through existing societal systems to achieve their prohomosexual objectives.

The "Christopher Street riot," or "Stonewall Riot," in New York City's Greenwich Village, on June 27, 1969, provided a major organizational impetus for the gay rights movement. It was an open confrontation between homosexuals and the police, who had raided a homosexual bar. That well-publicized homosexual protest generated the emotional symbolism out of which the Gay Liberation Front and similar activist organizations were organized in 1969 and the early 1970s.

Borrowing techniques from the more legitimate minority group movements of the 1960s, the prohomosexual activists developed a strategy to gain acceptability and proselytize under the guise of crusading for their rights. At the same time that legitimate social movements were formed to lobby for the civil rights of minority racial group members, these homosexual activists raised their cause as a plea for minority group rights for themselves. They tried to draw a parallel between themselves and victims of racial discrimination. Their strategy was to remove discussion of homosexuality from a moral framework, where questions regarding right or wrong would arise.

Are you as a parent aware of whether your children are being taught that "gay rights" are the same as civil rights in their school classrooms? That never happened when you were in school, because that was before the full development of the gay liberation movement, but your children are living in a different era.

THE HOMOSEXUAL PLAN FOR OUR CHILDREN

Prohomosexual activists seek not only to end violence and discrimination suffered by homosexuals but also to legitimatize homosexual relationships as an alternate life-style. Their goals are: (1) the removal of laws against private homosexual behavior between consenting persons *of any age*, (2) the enactment of laws to allow homosexuals equal opportunity for child custody, adopting children, and serving as foster parents, (3) the removal of legal statutes against homosexual solicitation and prostitution, and (4) the enactment of legislation to force public and private employers (such as schools) to hire openly practicing homosexuals to act as role models, to teach children that homosexuality is an acceptable alternative to the family life-style of the children's parents.[13] As responsible parents, we need to be aware of this extremist agenda and how it can influence our children.

The leaders of the homosexual revolt hope to convince secret homosexuals to "come out of the closet" and join their groups in order to obtain greater financial and political strength. Their purpose, in addition to changing the legal status of homosexuals, is to promote changes in sex-role stereotyping, to convince heterosexuals to adopt an accepting attitude toward homosexuality, and to change the low self-concept of homosexuals to "gay pride." The methods used to accomplish those aims include not only legal procedures and publishing of prohomosexual materials but also demonstrations, sit-ins, and social disruption.

FROM LIBERATION TO EXPLOITATION

The homosexuals are not all laughing. Why? One survey shows that only 2 percent of active homosexuals would want their own sons to be homosexuals.[14]

Parents should realize that homosexuality does pose a threat to children. There have been numerous court cases trying homosexual adults who enticed minors to participate in homosexual activities while they were photographed. The photographs were sold to distributors, and copies were made in pornographic magazines and films.

In one such large-scale operation in Nassau County, Long Island, four adults were arrested in connection with a "national recruitment program of young boys for the purpose of deviant sexual conduct."[15] According to the Nassau District Attorney, the boys and their families were bribed with expensive gifts. The boys ranged in age from seven to teenage. The investigation found that few of the boys had any inclination for homosexual conduct before they were contacted by these operators. Most of the boys had objected and would not participate in the sexual activity until after they had been bribed or seriously threatened.

Many gay activists advocate the removal of any "age discrimination" limiting homosexual behavior. Apparently they want to turn to younger and younger sex objects. That makes their demand for sexual relationships between "consenting adults" meaningless. To many homosexuals, the crusade to allow for freedom of homosexual expression to "consenting adults" is but a first step in a larger strategy to remove all social and legal restraints.

RHETORIC VERSUS REALITY

Gay activists often entice young people by promises of the warmth of same-sex affection, but it should be pointed out that homosexuals do not always get along well with one another. Many "macho" male homosexuals reject effeminate male homosexuals. Many male homosexuals have nothing to do with female homosexuals. Sado-masochistic homosexuals, transvestites, and other fetishistic homosexuals are frequently rejected and excluded by other homosexuals.

37

One of the difficulties encountered by leaders of the homosexual revolt is the antagonism toward subgroup members within the homosexual ranks. One strategy that has been successfully used by homosexual leaders, however, is to call the various homosexual subgroups together in a common protest of society's laws condemning their deviant practices. Thus some social cohesiveness within the homosexual community is generated by organizing against a common foe.

As a psychologist who has counseled scores of homosexuals, I have observed the pain suffered by individual homosexuals who have been manipulated by leaders of the homosexual revolt. Alone, the homosexual sees the deviance of other types of homosexuals, and he can even feel the need to change himself. But the homosexual leaders use the manipulative techniques of classical revolutionary strategies to achieve their own diabolical objectives, to the detriment of the individual suffering the effects of sexual perversion.

BACKLASH

Although homosexual leaders have managed to obtain a tremendous amount of media coverage of their activities, their efforts to legitimatize the homosexual life-style have so far met with only limited success. In Dade County, Florida, the County Commission passed an ordinance banning refusal of jobs based upon stated sexual preferences. Nationwide media attention resulted when citizen-parent activists succeeded in having the ordinance placed on a public ballot so they could reverse the County Commission vote. The citizens repealed the prohomosexual law in 1977, with a two-to-one margin, and reaffirmed their action in another vote two years later. This political event drew unprecedented public discussion. It often became a debate over society's right to maintain certain moral standards in schools and to prohibit sexual deviants from teaching children that the homosexual life-style is a respectable alternative to heterosexual family life. Similarly, as mentioned previously, citizen voters have removed ordinances or defeated proposed ordinances designed to promote homosexual life-styles in Boulder, Colorado; St. Paul, Minnesota; Wichita, Kansas; and Eugene, Oregon.

For many years, the New York City Council has voted against a hotly debated gay-rights bill. A different kind of initiative in California, designed to flush out schoolteachers suspected of homosexuality, was not approved by the voters, perhaps because its more negative approach appeared to infringe on normal rights of privacy.

The gay liberationists' zeal to recruit youth and to gain political power to promote the homosexual lifestyle clashes with commonly held moral and social values regarding childrearing. In 1977, the United States Supreme Court let stand rulings by state courts that homosexual behavior is immoral and that teachers may be dismissed for publicly acknowledging homosexuality as their preference.[16]

In May 1978, the United States Supreme Court further gave the states the signal that they may outlaw private homosexual acts between adults. In a test case involving a Jacksonville, North Carolina man, Eugene Enslin, who was convicted of violating the state's sodomy law and sentenced to a year in prison, the Supreme Court upheld the sentence. The Court supported a similar law in Virginia by upholding a lower court decision. The United States Supreme Court, therefore, interpreted the Constitution as allowing the states individually to decide whether to have laws against public or private homosexual behavior, and the court has upheld state definitions of homosexual behavior as immoral.

AMERICA: A MODERN SODOM?

The gay liberation movement has sprung up within our own lifetime. Homosexual activists seek to lure our children into a deceptive and destructive fantasy world that ignores the obvious physical, social, and moral boundaries of sexual expression. Everything that the gay activists are working for stands diametrically opposed to everything concerned parents stand for in seeking future family fulfillment for their children. Parents who are more aware of the tactics of homosexual activists will be better prepared to protect their own children from the ploys of these enemies of normal sexual development.

Genesis 19 describes the incident that took place in the city of Sodom, when two angels appearing as men visited a man named Lot. A group of men surrounded the house and demanded of Lot, "Where are the men who came to you tonight? Bring them out to us that we may have relations with them" (Genesis 19:5). The word translated "relations" is a Hebrew term that means "to know sexually," or "to have intercourse." Lot came out of the house and said, "Please, my brothers, do not act wickedly." Understanding their sexual interest and their aggressiveness, Lot tried to distract them from their homosexual intentions by offering his two virgin daughters, but they did not want women. The next day, God destroyed the cities of Sodom and Gomorrah as a punishment for their open homosexual sin (see also Genesis 13:13; Isaiah 3:9; Jeremiah 23:14). Jesus said that there will also be a future judgment of Sodom and Gomorrah (Matthew 10:15 and 11:23-24), and the apostle Jude wrote, "Just as Sodom and Gomorrah and the cities around them, since they in the same way as these indulged in gross immorality and went after strange flesh, are exhibited as an example, in undergoing the punishment of eternal fire" (Jude 7).

The destruction of the city of Sodom for unrestrained homosexual sin is God's example for the rest of us.

It is amazing that despite this clear warning, some twentieth-century Americans do not disapprove of the open gay activist movement in our country. Some go so far as to teach that the practice of homosexuality is completely compatible with Judeo-Christian values.[17] But what does the Bible say to us about such teaching?

> There will also be false teachers among you, who will secretly introduce destructive heresies, even denying the Master who bought them, bringing swift destruction upon themselves. And many will follow their sensuality, and because of them the way of the truth will be maligned; and in their greed they will exploit you with false words; their judgment from long ago is not idle, and their destruction is not asleep.
>
> For if God did not spare angels when they sinned, but cast them into hell and committed them to pits of darkness, reserved for judgment; and did not spare the ancient world, but preserved Noah, a preacher of righteousness, with seven others, when He brought a flood upon the world of the ungodly; and if He condemned the cities of Sodom and Gomorrah to destruction by reducing them to ashes, having made them an example to those who would live ungodly thereafter; and if He rescued righteous Lot, oppressed by the sensual conduct of unprincipled men (for by what he saw and heard that righteous man, while living among them, felt his righteous soul tormented day after day with their lawless deeds), then the Lord knows how to rescue the godly from temptation, and to keep the unrighteous under punishment for the day of judgment, and especially those who indulge the flesh in its corrupt desires and despise authority [2 Peter 2:1b-10a, italics added].

This biblical passage speaks of the certain condemnation of individuals who persist in following their corrupt desires, including open homosexual sinners like those in the ancient city of Sodom. Peter's prediction of future false teachers and advocates of sexual sin accurately describes twentieth-century advocates of gay liberation in America: "For speaking out arrogant words of vanity they entice by fleshly desires, by sensuality, those who barely escape from the ones who live in error, *promising them freedom while they themselves are slaves of corruption; for by what a man is overcome, by this he is enslaved*" (2 Peter 2:18-19, italics added).

1. See Frank M. duMas, *Gay Is Not Good* (Nashville: Nelson, 1979), chaps. 6-7. For examples of mental health professionals taking a prohomosexual value system, see A. Russell and R. C. Winkler, "Evaluation of Assertive Training and Homosexual Guidance Service Groups Designed to Improve Homosexual Functioning," *Journal of Consulting and Clinical Psychology* 45, 1 (1977): 1-13; and R. C. Winkler, "What Types of Sex-Role Behavior Should Behavior Modifiers Promote?" *Journal of Applied Behavior Analysis* 10 (1977): 549-52. Rebuttals to the prohomosexual arguments may be found in G. A. Rekers, "Atypical Gender Development and Psychosocial Adjustment," *Journal of Applied Behavior Analysis* 10 (1977): 559-71; and G. A. Rekers, "A Priori Values and Research on Homosexuality," *American Psychologist* 33 (1978): 510-12.
2. Michael Braun and George A. Rekers, *The Christian in an Age of Sexual Eclipse* (Wheaton, Ill.: Tyndale, 1981), chap. 2. See also *Humanist Manifesto I and II* (Buffalo: Prometheus, 1973), p. 18.
3. *Humanist Manifesto I and II*, pp. 15-18. See also Braun and Rekers, chap. 4.
4. Nancy Lehmann and Helen Sullinger, *The Document: Declaration of Feminism* (Minneapolis: Powderhorn Station, 1972), pp. 13-14; Mary Samis, Tish Sommers, Marjorie Suelzie, and Nan Wood, eds., *Revolution: Tomorrow Is NOW* (Washington, D.C.: National Organization for Women, 1977); *National Plan of Action Adopted at National Women's Conference, November 18-21, 1977, Houston, Texas* (Washington, D.C.: International Women's Year Commission, 1977). See also Braun and Rekers, chap. 7.
5. See *Humanist Manifesto I and II* for an example of how current terminology reflects changing attitudes toward sexual morality; see also Braun and Rekers, chap. 6, for a critique of contemporary arguments against marital fidelity.
6. Lehmann and Sullinger, p. 809; *National Plan of Action*, p. 27.
7. Lehmann and Sullinger, p. 11.
8. Ibid.
9. *Humanist Manifesto I and II*, p. 13.
10. Ibid., p. 17.
11. Ibid., pp. 16, 18.

12. S. F. Morin, "Heterosexual Bias in Psychological Research on Lesbianism and Male Homosexuality," *American Psychologist* 32 (1977): 629-37. See also a rebuttal to Morin's article in G. A. Rekers, "A Priori Values and Research on Homosexuality," *American Psychologist* 33 (1978): 510-12.

13. These goals were endorsed, for example, by the American Psychological Association, in *Removing the Stigma—Final Report of the Board of Social and Ethical Responsibility for Psychology's Task Force on the Status of Lesbian and Gay Male Psychologists* (Washington, D.C.: APA, 1981). See also *APA Committee on Gay Concerns* (Washington, D.C.: APA, 1981); Stephen F. Morin and Stephen J. Schultz, "The Gay Movement and the Rights of Children," *Journal of Social Issues* 34, no. 2 (1978): 137-48; D. Teal, *The Gay Militants* (New York: Stein and Day, 1971); K. Jay and A. Young, eds., *Out of the Closet: Voices of the Gay Liberation* (New York: Douglas, 1972); K. Tobin and R. Wicker, *The Gay Crusaders* (New York: Paperback Library, 1971); C. Klein, "Homosexual Parents," in *The Single Parent Experience* (New York: Walker, 1973): W. Aaron, *Straight—A Homosexual Talks About His Homosexual Past* (New York: Doubleday, 1972); Dorothy I. Riddle, "Relating to Children: Gays as Role Models," *Journal of Social Issues* 34 no. 3 (1978): 38-58.

14. Cited in John W. Drakeford and Jack Hamm, *Pornography: The Sexual Mirage* (Nashville: Nelson, 1973).

15. "New York: White Slavery, 1972," *Time,* 5 June 1972, p. 24; Drakeford and Hamm, pp. 82-83.

16. United Press International, "Decisions: Court Enters Controversial Areas," *Florida Times-Union,* 4 October 1977, p. 1.

17. See Ronald M. Enroth and Gerald E. Jamison, *The Gay Church* (Grand Rapids: Eerdmans, 1974), for a critique of gay theology.

3

Is Gay OK?

The noisy crowd gathered at noon in the central Meyerhoff Park courtyard of the UCLA campus. The rally had been organized by a hastily formed group calling itself "Coalition Against the Dehumanization of Children"—an ad hoc committee composed of some members of the Gay Student Union, the Women's Resource Center, and others.[1] Four speakers addressed the assembled students to protest against me and my colleagues, who directed a UCLA Psychology Clinic program for treating childhood gender problems. The speakers threw out such accusations and complaints as, "They are training children to be androids"; "This treatment oppresses kids"; "The program conditions the children to aggressive, war-like behavior"; "It is not proper to treat the victims of society."

Clearly, the gay liberation groups in Los Angeles were alarmed and angry about this federally-funded program, established to provide preventative treatment to children at high risk for developing transsexualism, transvestism, or homosexuality.

The incident raised several questions about the na-

45

ture of homosexuality. Should doctors consider homosexuality a mental illness warranting clinical treatment? Or is it something that develops naturally and should be left alone? Is there a release from homosexuality?

Those are not just political questions; they are very personal questions as well, as illustrated in the following case.

"JOHN"

After a few preliminaries, Pastor Thomas got to the point of his telephone call. "John is sixteen years old and he has been aware of his homosexual interests since he was nine. He's afraid to tell his parents about it, for fear that they might kick him out of the house. He couldn't tell his own pastor about his sexual problem because his pastor's son is one of the teenage boys that John has a crush on. John desperately wants to overcome homosexuality. I recommended that he see you."

Two days later, John came for his first visit. He was a good-looking, blond boy of medium build. He told me that he had had strong homosexual interests for seven years, and he estimated that in the last year he had been involved in homosexual relations with other teenagers about three times a month.

After reviewing many of his homosexual experiences, John confessed: "For a long time, I've felt guilty about either being this way or for having done these things. I realize what I have done was wrong."

Of other boys who drew him into sexual activity as a child, John said, "I feel like I got taken advantage of, but it's not their fault that I kept doing this after I knew it was wrong.

"It's like with Ted now. I wouldn't mind going to bed with him, but I would also like not to want to. Ted doesn't seem to be bothered by how I feel about him, but maybe it's because he's just affectionate toward everyone."

John asked many questions about how he could overcome his homosexual temptations. He wanted to know if it would ever be possible for him to marry successfully and to have his emotional needs cared for so that he would not be constantly seeking attention and sexual favors from other males.

He strongly believed that his homosexual behavior was disapproved by God, his pastor, and his church, but he was confused by his pastor's son's apparent acceptance of him as a homosexual. Was it just that Ted accepted him in Christian love, regardless of his moral problems?

Then John finally sputtered out his biggest question: "Am I—is this mentally ill, or what? Am I sick, or what?" He wanted to know how doctors would diagnose his condition, and he sought assurances that our clinic would support his goal to overcome homosexual temptations. What do doctors say about homosexuality? Is gay OK?

Is Homosexuality Abnormal?

From the earliest days of psychiatry, a loving heterosexual relationship in marriage has been considered the norm against which other sexual practices have been measured in defining sexual deviation. The American Psychiatric Association (APA) publishes the *Diagnostic and Statistical Manual of Mental Disorders*, which is routinely used by professionals to classify psychiatric disturbances. The second edition of the *Manual*, published in 1968, included the following diagnosis:

302. Sexual Deviations
This category is for individuals whose sexual interests are

directed primarily toward objects other than people of the opposite sex, toward sexual acts . . . performed under bizarre circumstances. . . . Even though many find their practices distasteful, they remain unable to substitute normal sexual behavior for them. This diagnosis is not appropriate for individuals who perform deviant sexual acts because normal sexual objects are not available to them.[2]

Homosexuality was the first deviation listed in this category.

PERVERSION IN PSYCHIATRY

On December 15, 1973, the homosexual liberationists were successful in lobbying for their cause at the annual APA meeting. They persuaded a majority of the APA Board of Trustees to remove homosexuality from their list of mental disorders. To replace homosexuality, the APA created the new diagnosis of "Sexual orientation disturbance (Homosexuality)," which can be used by doctors to classify a patient who has psychological conflicts over his homosexual behavior.

This is for individuals whose sexual interests are directed primarily toward people of the same sex and who are either disturbed by, in conflict with, or wish to change their sexual orientation. This diagnostic category is distinguished from homosexuality, which by itself does not constitute a psychiatric disorder. Homosexuality per se is one form of sexual behavior, and with other forms of sexual behavior which are not by themselves psychiatric disorders, are not listed in this nomenclature.[3]

In essence, if a person has no conscious or unconscious conflict over his homosexuality, he is not diagnosed as mentally ill.

Along with the modified classification, the APA issued an official statement declaring, "This is not to say that homosexuality is 'normal' or that it is as desirable as heterosexuality."

In 1980, the American Psychiatric Association issued the third edition of their diagnostic manual. It includes the new category "Ego-dystonic homosexuality," which also assumes that it is not homosexuality per se that constitutes mental illness. The diagnostic criteria for "ego-dystonic homosexuality" are:

A. The individual complains that heterosexual arousal is persistently absent or weak and significantly interferes with initiating or maintaining wanted heterosexual relationships.
B. There is a sustained pattern of homosexual arousal that the individual explicitly states has been unwanted and a persistent source of distress.[4]

The manual states, "When the disorder is present in an adult, usually there is a strong desire to be able to have children and family life."[5] It also notes, "Loneliness is particularly common. In addition, guilt, shame, anxiety, and depression may be present."[6]

In explaining the change from the previous diagnosis of homosexuality as a disorder, the 1980 *Diagnostic and Statistical Manual* says:

Ego-dystonic Homosexuality is not included as a Paraphilia in DSM-III, in contrast to the inclusion of both Homosexuality and Sexual Orientation Disturbance in DSM-II as Sexual Deviations, because in DSM-III the Paraphilias are limited to conditions that are associated with (1) preference for the use of a nonhuman object for sexual arousal, (2) repetitive sexual activity with humans involving real or simulated suffering or humiliation, or (3) repetitive sexual activity with non-consenting or *inappropriate partners* [italics added].[7]

(The reader will note the arbitrary decision that a same-sexed partner is *not* "inappropriate.")

Similarly, without first polling the membership, a handful of officials in the American Psychological Association mandated prohomosexual values for the profession. The American Psychological Association's "Resolutions on Gay Rights" were adopted in January 1975 by a small group of association office-holders, who voted to support the American Psychiatric Association's removal of homosexuality from the official list of mental disorders. The policy also stated, "Further, the American Psychological Association urges all mental health professionals to take the lead in removing the stigma of mental illness that has long been associated with homosexual orientations."[8]

On September 5, 1976, the Council of Representatives of the American Psychological Association adopted the following resolution, initiated by the "Task Force on the Status of Lesbian and Gay Psychologists of the Board of Social and Ethical Responsibility for Psychology": "The sex, gender identity, or sexual orientation of natural, or prospective adoptive or foster parents should not be the sole or primary variable considered in custody or placement cases."[9] In other words, the American Psychological Association now holds that a homosexual couple should not be ruled out on account of their homosexuality if they apply to adopt or foster-parent a child.

The American Psychological Association leadership has funded both a "Task Force on the Status of Lesbian and Gay Psychologists," and a continuing "Committee on Gay Concerns." One member of the task force defined gay in terms of a value system: "The emerging definition of 'gay' or 'lesbian' is different from that of 'homosexual.' The term *gay*, like the terms *black*, *Chicano*, and *woman*, connotes a value system as well as designates group membership. Gay is proud, angry, open, visible, political, healthy, and all the positive things that *homosexual* is not."[10]

So we see that the American Psychological Association has not taken a neutral position but has officially approved and funded a prohomosexual position opposed to historic Judeo-Christian values.[11]

One cannot escape the irony of those decisions—or perhaps the satanic subtlety of them. A few generations ago humanists were successful in convincing our society no longer to call a homosexual a pervert and a culprit in acts of moral evil. No, he should be "humanely" considered sick, and in need of treatment for his illness. Now we have moved to stage 2: the homosexual should no longer be considered even sick. In less than a century, many in our society have moved from considering homosexuality a moral evil, to considering it a sickness, to denying that it has any moral or pathological significance at all.

This new concept of abnormality discards the concept that a norm exists outside the person; instead, the individual establishes his or her own norm. If the individual independently chooses homosexuality and is not disturbed, conflicted with, or wishing to change this choice, then he is diagnosed as mentally healthy. Internal conflict alone becomes the criterion for considering homosexuality a psychiatric disorder, with no reference to any norm of reality outside the individual.

Now that the American Psychiatric Association. has abandoned its formerly logical underpinnings of comparing a patient to a norm outside himself, all psychiatric disorders may be subject to reanalysis. What if one afflicted with any other disorder, such as paranoia, did not wish to change? Would he thereby be considered "normal"? Why single out homosexuality for special treatment? The reason is that the gay liberation lobby is a political reality, promoted by humanistic rhetoric in the media.

But what do the majority of the psychiatrists in the APA really think? What do practicing psychiatrists do when they encounter a homosexual patient? Do they consider him abnormal?

In 1977, the medical journal *Medical Aspects of Human Sexuality* conducted a major survey of APA members and found that 69 percent of the psychiatrists responding judged homosexuality as pathological rather than normal, with 13 percent uncertain. That means that the politically active minority crusading against listing homosexuality as a mental disorder constituted perhaps less than 18 percent of the APA membership. The revised policies were published before the full membership could review or approve them.

Here are the answers that the psychiatrists gave to a number of questions about homosexuality:[12]

Are homosexual men generally less happy than others?

Yes 73%   No 26%

Are homosexual men generally less capable than heterosexual men of mature, loving relationships?

Yes 60%   No 39%

Are lesbian women less capable than heterosexual women of mature, loving relationships?

Yes 55%   No 43%

Are homosexuals' problems in living a result of personal conflicts more than of stigmatization?

Yes 70%   No 28%

Can bisexuals have successful heterosexual marriages?

Usually 21%   Occasionally 65%   Almost never 12%

Are homosexuals generally more creative than heterosexuals?

Yes 22%   No 74%

Are homosexuals generally a greater risk than het-

erosexuals to hold positions of great responsibility?
Yes 43%   No 54%

Is Homosexuality Healthy?

Although a minority of psychiatric physicians crusade for acceptance of their decision that no psychiatric treatment should be offered for homosexuality per se, the rest of the medical profession is acutely aware of the unhealthy consequences of homosexual behavior.

Serious consequences to health, resulting from a promiscuous homosexual life-style, bear testimony to the inviolability of biological laws. The medical profession is most likely to be involved with practicing homosexuals in diagnosing and treating venereal disease.

It has been reported that homosexuals tend to have more sexual contacts than heterosexuals and that they have an associated higher rate of venereal disease, especially rectal gonorrhea and venereal warts.[13] In fact, many public health studies have pointed out that the homosexual community is the major reservoir for venereal diseases.[14] Drs. Felman and Morrison of the New York City Health Department[15] report that a homosexual male's chances of contracting syphilis are five times that of a heterosexual male. They also point out that because many homosexuals do not tell their physicians that they are engaging in homosexual practices, the physician often fails to make the appropriate diagnostic tests for such infections.

In a study of venereal disease in 200 male homosexuals in New York, Drs. Sohn and Robilotti[16] stated, "The public health implications of male homosexual behavior are very important. These patients may be employed as food handlers or in other roles where they could come into contact with others and be a source of spread of amebiasis, hepatitis and shigellosis" (diseases of the gastro-intestinal tract). Such infections are considered venereal diseases because they are passed from person to person through sexual contact. Investigators at the San Francisco Department of Public Health concluded that cases of shigellosis, amebiasis, and viral hepatitis A and B are most commonly transmitted by people who have adopted "alternative sexual lifestyles."[17]

Another study of 198 practicing homosexuals found hepatitis B in much higher incidence among homosexuals than among heterosexuals. The risk of infection increased with the number of sexual partners.[18] Typhoid fever also has been transmitted sexually between homosexuals.[19]

The epidemic proportion of disease among homosexuals diverts medical skills and facilities from other diseases and their treatment. For that reason, some doctors have declared that society has an economic stake in the "private" sexual behavior between consenting adults, particularly if we consider the fact that tax revenues must be raised to provide medical treatment for the increase of venereal disease in modern industrialized nations. Considering only the public health issues involved, we must conclude that homosexual conduct is a matter of profound social impact.

With that information alone, we might expect doctors in psychology and psychiatry as well as medical doctors to conclude that faithful, married heterosexuality is a norm consistent with reality, whereas all types of promiscuous sexual behavior violate that reality —and are therefore abnormal.

THE SEARCH FOR TRUTH ABOUT HOMOSEXUALITY

An honest, scholarly search for the truth about

homosexuality should not stop with psychological or medical information alone. Wise professionals should also consider evidence for moral truth as well. The Bible teaches that people are foolish if they deny God's reality and live their lives as though He were not there:[20]

> For a fool speaks nonsense, and his heart inclines toward wickedness, to practice ungodliness and to speak error against the LORD, to keep the hungry person unsatisfied and to withhold drink from the thirsty [Isaiah 32:6].
> The fool has said in his heart, "There is no God." They are corrupt, they have committed abominable deeds [Psalm 14:1a].
> The wicked, in the haughtiness of his countenance, does not seek Him. All his thoughts are, "There is no God" [Psalm 10:4].

The Bible teaches that truth about creation should be sought with the Creator in mind. "The fear of the LORD is the beginning of knowledge; fools despise wisdom and instruction" (Proverbs 1:7).

What happens when psychologists and psychiatrists search for truth about homosexuality but close the door to any possibility of information from the Creator of the human race? What happens if scholars deliberately discard all moral evidence as irrelevant to their professional judgments?

Romans 1:18-21 describes the consequences of suppressing truth revealed by the Creator:

> For the wrath of God is revealed from heaven against all ungodliness and unrighteousness of men, who suppress the truth in unrighteousness, because that which is known about God is evident within them; for God made it evident to them. For since the creation of the world His invisible attributes, His eternal power and divine nature, have been clearly seen, being understood through what has been made, so that they are without excuse. For even

55

though they knew God, they did not honor Him as God, or give thanks; but they became futile in their speculations, and their foolish heart was darkened.

Those verses indicate that the existence of God is evident within each person, so psychologists and psychiatrists who proceed as though He does not exist are deliberately suppressing truth. To search for truth about homosexuality in psychology and psychiatry while ignoring God will result in futile and foolish speculations.

Can we trust the conclusions of such a secularized psychology and psychiatry to be wise? *"Professing to be wise, they became fools,* and exchanged the glory of the incorruptible God for an image in the form of corruptible man and of birds and four-footed animals and crawling creatures" (Romans 1:22-23, italics added).

When individuals live in deliberate, practical ignorance of God, what is the consequence to their sexual lives?

Therefore God gave them over in the lusts of their hearts to impurity, that their bodies might be dishonored among them. *For they exchanged the truth of God for a lie,* and worshiped and *served the creature* rather than the Creator, who is blessed forever. Amen.

For this reason, God gave them over to degrading passions; for their women exchanged the natural function for that which is unnatural, and in the same way also the men abandoned the natural function of the woman and burned in their desire toward one another, men with men committing indecent acts and receiving in their own persons the due penalty of their error. And just as they did not see fit to acknowledge God any longer, God gave them over to a depraved mind, to do those things which are not proper. . . . And although they know the ordinance of God, that those who practice such things are worthy of death, they not only do the same, but also give hearty approval to those who practice them [Romans 1:24-28, 32, italics added].

Those verses describe the shift from a God-centered world view to a humanistic world view, which places the individual at the center of the universe.[21] We have seen a fulfillment of these verses in the actions taken by the American Psychological Association and the American Psychiatric Association, which have declared their own "truth" about homosexuality while suppressing truth from the Creator. As a result, the homosexual minorities in those associations have succeeded in openly embracing homosexual practices for themselves and in giving "hearty approval to those who practice them."

What should be the concerned parent's attitude toward the atheistic or agnostic views of some mental health professionals? Is there valuable wisdom to be gained from the doctor who endorses homosexuality as normal? Scripture teaches us clearly: "For the wisdom of this world is foolishness before God. For it is written, 'He is THE ONE WHO CATCHES THE WISE IN THEIR CRAFTINESS'; and again, 'THE LORD KNOWS THE REASONINGS of the wise, THAT THEY ARE USELESS' " (1 Corinthians 3:19-20).

---

1. For accounts of this incident, see Geoff Quinn, "Sex Role Program Opposed," U.C.L.A. Daily Bruin, 29 January 1975; John Wilson, "Male-Gram," U.C.L.A. Daily Bruin, 4 February 1975; Patrick Healy and Geoff Quinn, "1984 Is Here—Gender Program Rapped," U.C.L.A. Daily Bruin, 7 February 1975.
2. American Psychiatric Association, Diagnostic and Statistical Manual of Mental Disorders, 2d ed. (Washington, D.C.: APA, 1968), p. 44. See Frank M. duMas, Gay Is Not Good (Nashville: Nelson, 1979), pp. 126-36, 243-57, for a critique of the process by which this change was made.
3. American Psychiatric Association, p. 44. The footnote to this change read, "This term and its definition are inconsistent with the change in thinking that led to the substitution of Sexual Orientation Disturbance for Homosexuality in the list below. However, since no specific recommendations were made for changing this category or its definition, this category remains unchanged for the time being" (p. 44).
4. American Psychiatric Association, Diagnostic and Statistical Manual of Mental Disorders, 3d ed. (Washington, D.C.: APA, 1980), p. 282.
5. Ibid., p. 281.
6. Ibid.

7. Ibid., p. 380.
8. American Psychological Association, *Removing the Stigma —Final Report of the Board of Social and Ethical Responsibility for Psychology's Task Force on the Status of Lesbian and Gay Male Psychologists* (Washington, D.C.: APA, 1979), p. 2.
9. Ibid., p. 4.
10. Stephen F. Morin, "Heterosexual Bias in Psychological Research on Homosexuality," *American Psychologist* 32 (1977): 629-37.
11. G. A. Rekers, "A Priori Values and Research on Homosexuality," *American Psychologist* 33 (1978): 510-12.
12. Harold I. Lief, "Sexual Survey Number 4: Current Thinking on Homosexuality," *Medical Aspects of Human Sexuality* 2 (1977): 110-11.
13. R. B. Mauer, "Health Care and the Gay Community," *Postgraduate Medicine* 58, 1 (July 1975): 127-30. Involvement in homosexual behavior has been reported to be a risk factor for many different diseases. Numerous articles are published in medical journals each year documenting the spread of various diseases by homosexual activity. Here are just a few selected examples of this growing body of scientific reports: S. Vaisrub, "Homosexuality—A Risk Factor in Infectious Disease" (editorial), *Journal of the American Medical Association* 238, 13 (26 September 1977): 1402; D. Goldmeir, "Proctitis and Herpes Simplex Virus in Homosexual Men," *British Journal of Venereal Disease* 56, 2 (April 1980): 111-14; K. B. Hymes, et al., "Kaposi's Sarcoma in Homosexual Men—A Report of Eight Cases," *Lancet* 2 Pt 1, 8247 (19 September 1981): 598-600; R. D. Leach,et al., "Carcinoma of the Rectum in Male Homosexuals," *Journal of the Royal Society of Medicine* 74, 7 (July 1981): 490-91; J. D. Meyers, et al., "Giardia Lamblia Infection in Homosexual Men," *British Journal of Venereal Disease* 53, 1 (February 1977): 54-55; D. Mildvan, et al., "Venereal Transmission of Enteric Pathogens in Male Homosexuals: Two Case Reports," *Journal of the American Medical Association* 238, 13 (26 September 1977): 1387-89; P. L. Samarasinghe, "Herpetic Proctitis and Sacral Radiomyelopathy—A Hazard for Homosexual Men," *British Medical Journal* 2, 6186 (11 August 1979): 365-66.
14. Michael Braun and George A. Rekers, *The Christian in an Age of Sexual Eclipse* (Wheaton, Ill.: Tyndale, 1981), chap. 6.
15. Y. M. Felman and J. M. Morrison, "Examining Homosexual Males for Sexually Transmitted Diseases," *Journal of the American Medical Association* 238, 19 (1977): 2046-47. See also, e.g., the following articles: H. H. Handsfield, "Sexually Transmitted Diseases," *American Journal of Public Health* 71, 9 (September 1981): 989-90; W. F. Owen, Jr., "Sexually Transmitted Diseases and Traumatic Problems in Homosexual Men," *Annals of Internal Medicine* 92, 6 (June 1980): 805-8.
16. N. Sohn and J. G. Robilotti, Jr., "The Gay Bowel Syndrome: A Review of Colonic and Rectal Conditions in 200 Male Homosexuals," *American Journal of Gastroenterology* 67, 5 (May 1977): 478-84. Every year, medical researchers publish numerous new articles such as this on the public health problems caused by promiscuous homosexual behavior. Here are just a few recent examples from among many published studies that document this fact: D. Goldmeier, et al., "Isolation of Chlamydia Trachomatis from Throat and Rectum of Homosexual Men," *British Journal of Venereal Disease* 53, 3 (June 1977): 184-85; T. C. Quinn, L. Corey, R. G. Chaffee, M. D. Schuffer, F. P. Brancato, and K. K. Holmes, "The

Etiology of Anorectal Infections in Homosexual Men," *American Journal of Medicine* 71, 3 (September 1981): 395-406; F. C. Wolf, et al., "Intensive Screening for Gonorrhea, Syphilis, and Hepatitis B in a Gay Bathhouse Does Not Lower the Prevalence Infection," *Sexually Transmitted Diseases* 7, 2 (April-June 1980): 49-52.

17. S. K. Dritz, T. E. Ainsworth, A. Bach, et al., "Patterns of Sexually Transmitted Enteric Diseases in a City," *Lancet* 2, 8027 (2 July 1977): 3-4. These diseases have also been reported to be spread by homosexual relationships in many other cities. See, e.g., the following article: M. J. Schmerin, et al., "Amebiasis: An Increasing Problem Among Homosexuals in New York City," *Journal of the American Medical Association* 238, 13 (26 September 1977): 1386-87.

18. K. S. Lim, V. T. Wong, K. W. Fulford, et al., "Role of Sexual and Non-Sexual Practices in the Transmission of Hepatitis B," *British Journal of Venereal Disease* 53, 3 (June 1977): 190-92. Many medical articles have been published on the various liver diseases spread by homosexual acts, including both hepatitis A and B. See, e.g., the following articles: L. Corey, et al., "Sexual Transmission of Hepatitis A in Homosexual Men: Incidence and Mechanism," *New England Journal of Medicine* 302, 8 (21 February 1980): 435-38; P. Skinhoj, "Chronic Hepatitis B Infection in Male Homosexuals," *Journal of Clinical Pathology* 32, 8 (August 1979): 783-85.

19. S. K. Dritz and E. H. Branff, "Sexually Transmitted Typhoid Fever," *New England Journal of Medicine* 296, 23 (9 June 1977): 1359-60.

20. See also Francis A. Schaeffer, *The God Who Is There* (Downers Grove, Ill.: Inter-Varsity, 1968); Francis A. Schaeffer, *He Is There and He Is Not Silent* (Wheaton, Ill.: Tyndale, 1972).

21. See also Francis A. Schaeffer, *How Should We Then Live?* (Old Tappan, N.J.: Revell, 1976).

59

II
The Trap of Homosexuality

4

What Causes Homosexual Tendencies?

When Danny was eight years old, his adoptive parents brought him to my office with questions about his future development. They wanted to provide a healthy family life for him, in contrast to that which he had experienced during his first seven years, when he was subjected to physical and mental abuse and to homosexual activities initiated by his father.

On the third day in his new home, Danny had come to talk with his new mother. It was clear that although he had something important to say, it was difficult for him to do so. His new mother took him into his bedroom and said, "Danny, we know that your daddy did some things to your body that were not good for him or for you. Here in our home, you don't have to be afraid of that kind of thing anymore. We just wanted you to know that we know what happened, and we know it wasn't your fault, so it's OK."

As she was telling him that, a tear trickled down his cheek, and he reached up and hugged her. He did not say a word then, but later he was able to tell her some of what had happened with his former father.

Several weeks later, Danny initiated some homosexual activity with another boy in the neighborhood. When his mother asked him about it, he said, "Well, Mom, sometimes I get this in my mind. I try to forget what's happened to me, but when I get it in my mind, it's all I can think about."

Because of this early childhood history and the recent homosexual incident, Danny's new mother wanted to know how best to help him. She had many pressing questions: What exactly is homosexuality? What are homosexual temptations? Is Danny responsible for his homosexual urges? Will Danny's unfortunate early experience doom him to homosexuality? Or can he grow up to a normal, heterosexual family life?

Not all adult homosexuals started out with the kind of sexual abuse Danny had experienced as a little boy; there are many different pathways to the dead end of homosexual involvement.

CAN WE BLAME BIOLOGY?

Nineteenth-century theories about the causes of homosexuality mistakenly assumed that the condition was biological. It is true that sexual behavior in lower animals is instinctual, governed by the hormonal system, and sexual behavior in the higher mammals is influenced by both hormones and learning. But in humans, research has shown that the direction of sexual preference is apparently the product of learning experiences rather than of biological factors.

Many gay liberationists glibly claim that being gay or straight is like being left-handed or right-handed. But scientific facts are to the contrary. Left-handedness or righthandedness is determined by an inborn dominance of one half of the brain over the other; therefore, left- or right-handedness is a biologically caused predisposition. However, homosexual behavior patterns have *not* been found to be caused by such a simple, straightforward biological mechanism. In fact, not even homosexual temptation itself has been positively linked in any way with any biological cause.[1] In experiments where doses of male hormones were given to male homosexuals, only the intensity of their sexual desire and arousal changed, not their sex-object choice. Male hormones just increase homosexual desire in homosexual men. Although a few recent studies have suggested the possibility of some minor biological correlates with homosexuality, none have demonstrated a biological condition as directly causing homosexual behavior.[2]

If there is no biological cause that forces a person to engage in homosexual behavior, then the people who are involved in homosexual acts are those who have homosexual temptations and yield to them. This leads us to two basic questions:

(1) What makes a person vulnerable to homosexual temptations?

(2) What is the difference between the person who resists and the person who gives in to homosexual temptation?

People who experience homosexual temptations are said to have homosexual tendencies. A wide variety of social learning experiences evidently contribute to vulnerability to homosexual temptation. Because there are many different types of homosexuality, there are many different combinations of factors that can contribute to homosexual temptation, lust, and behavior.

THERE'S NO PLACE LIKE HOME

How a child is raised in a family has much to do with his or her vulnerability to temptation. The first five years of a child's life are usually those in which the parents can have a virtual monopoly on influencing their children. If 95 percent of the young child's day is spent with his parents, those parents will be molding and shaping a little boy's or little girl's personality, resulting in long-term effects.

Certainly, between the ages of five and eighteen years, the child can be significantly influenced by the parents; indeed, it is necessary for the parents to continue to be a positive influence upon the child during later childhood and the adolescent years in order to insure a normal heterosexual family adjustment for that child. However, the tremendous influence that they can have during the child's first five years of life is something that may never again be enjoyed to the same extent.

In a stable and successful home, parents can be the single most important influence upon a child's successfully developing normal heterosexual adjustment in spite of all kinds of perverted influences from outside the family. But serious problems in the family can make the child vulnerable to developing sexual deviations in adulthood, especially if his friends, the media, or the school provide encouragement to that deviance. It is true that in some cases, constructive outside influences can override the negative effects of an unfortunate family life, but the best insurance against sexual deviation is a healthy family life.

FAMILY INFLUENCES ON HOMOSEXUALITY

There have been many studies on how normal boys and girls develop their sexual identity and their appropriate sexual roles. Over and over, the father has been found to be the parent who has the greatest influence on the sex-appropriate behavior development in children.[3] The father's nurturance of his children and his leadership in family life turn out to be critical characteristics in the development of normal sexual

66

identity in sons and daughters. When fathers are either physically or psychologically absent from the home, their children may suffer major problems in their sexual role adjustment.[4]

Most of the studies that have related homosexuality with family environment have been based on information gathered from extensive interviews with adult homosexuals and, in many cases, with their immediate family members as well. From such studies, we have learned about the influence of family life on one's sexual adjustment in adulthood.[5]

What kind of families do homosexuals come from? What information do we have from adults who now engage in homosexual activities? At the outset, we need to realize that their reports in no way prove that certain early family experiences *cause* the homosexual behavior; an adult can choose, daily, whether he or she will engage in a particular sexual behavior. But the information can suggest what family background might have made one child more vulnerable to homosexual temptation than another.

Certain kinds of families can leave a child with unresolved emotional conflicts or with feelings that tempt him to pursue a shortcut to intimacy by having sexual relations with a person of the same sex. But because of the uniqueness of individual make-up, our discussion here can only be in generalities that will not necessarily apply to every case.

Many studies of homosexual patients[6] as well as of nonpatient homosexuals[7] have established a classic pattern of background family relations. The most frequent family pattern reported from the male homosexual includes a binding, intimate mother in combination with a hostile, detached father.

The fathers of homosexual sons are reported to be less affectionate than fathers of heterosexual sons.[8] In one study of forty homosexual men, there was not a single case in which the man reported having had an affectionate relationship with his father.[9] In fact, homosexual men often fear and even hate their fathers.[10] (In studies where the reports of effeminate males have been compared to those of more masculine homosexual males, the more masculine homosexuals have been found to have had somewhat better relationships with their fathers.)[11]

The fathers of homosexual sons are most often described as being aloof, hostile, and rejecting. More than four-fifths of adult male homosexuals report that their fathers were physically or psychologically absent from their homes while they were growing up. In addition, those fathers rarely made any effort to protect their sons from the unusual influence of an overly close mother.[12]

The fathers of homosexual men have been found to be indifferent and uninvolved with their families. Such fathers are often perceived by their sons as being rejecting and critical of their sons' lack of interest in typically masculine activities. In a majority of cases, fathers had left the decision-making in the home to the mothers. Significantly, only 13 percent of the homosexuals in a controlled study identified with their fathers in comparison to 66 percent of the heterosexual men in the same study.[13]

Even clinical studies of *heterosexual* males reveal that when fathers are either physically or psychologically absent, boys experience some difficulty in their psychosexual development. This difficulty is even more pronounced in the case of homosexual sons. In the many clinical studies of homosexuals, the characteristics of the father that would foster normal psychosexual adjustment—nurturance, affection, and active leadership in the family—are all notably lacking. Many homosexual men report that their homes in childhood were mother-dominated.[14] In such homes, neither the mother nor the father typically encouraged masculine activities or attitudes in their sons.[15]

In families like these, vulnerability to homosexual temptation may occur when disturbances in a child's relationships with his father and mother result in unfulfilled emotional needs. The resultant emotional problems and conflicts can make the child vulnerable to homosexual attraction.[16] Vulnerability to homosexual temptation can also result if the parent tells the child that homosexuality is OK or, more obviously, if parents involve their children in incestuous homosexual acts.

OTHER INFLUENCES

Unfortunately, parents do not control every influence on their children. Concerned parents could avoid all kinds of family problems and their children might still grow up with homosexual tendencies. How does that happen? In some cases it happens because parents are not the only influence on their child. Other factors that may contribute to the development of homosexual temptation include prohomosexual values promoted by television or reading material, "values clarification" in schools (or even in some churches) teaching sexual relativism, or propaganda by gay liberationists.

In other cases, homosexual temptations arise from strong peer group influence to engage in homosexual activities.

Some children may label themselves homosexual after an experience with an older person who initiates homosexual activity. That can lead to withdrawal from normal dating experiences in the teenage years.

In other young people, negative experience with a person of the opposite sex leads to aversion to relating normally, opening the door to an abnormal desire for sexual intimacy with someone of the same sex. Similarly, some teenagers get involved in premarital heterosexual encounters that turn out to be negative and guilt producing. They then develop a generalized fear of normal dating and marriage and direct their sexual interests toward homosexual objects instead.

VULNERABILITY IS NOT DETERMINISM

There are a variety of psychological experiences that may make a person vulnerable to developing a homosexual interest. (Even that speculation, however, has not been proved by any scientific experiment.) The fact that individuals with homosexual practices come from such diverse family and personal backgrounds somewhat undermines the classical theory that *all* homosexuals were made vulnerable to temptation by a dominant mother and a weak, ineffectual father.[17]

The recent finding by the Institute for Sex Research (Indiana University) that there are many different kinds of homosexuality, each stemming from many different backgrounds,[18] lends credibility to the observation that homosexual practices, in the end, are chosen behavior.

Commenting on recent investigations of homosexuality, one researcher emphasized the "need to conceive of sexual patterns as not simply the result of past influences, but as *goal-directed behavior* involving a broad range of reinforcements in the present *which are not entirely related to residues of the past* and which involve more than the fulfillment of sexual needs."[19]

In psychological literature, there are more unanswered questions about what causes homosexuality than there are definitive answers. No biological, social, or psychological factor or combination of factors has been found to *force* a person to choose to engage in homosexual behavior.

70

Even though parents cannot absolutely control the influences on their children or the choices their children make, they do have a responsibility to give their children as firm a foundation as possible by providing them with a healthy family life. The following chapter will explore ways in which this can be done.

1. Frank M. duMas, *Gay Is Not Good* (Nashville: Nelson, 1979).
2. Ibid. See also A. P. Bell and M. S. Weinberg, *Homosexualities* (New York: Simon & Schuster, 1978).
3. B. I. Fagot, "Sex Differences in Toddlers' Behavior and Parental Reaction," *Developmental Psychology*, 19 (1974): 554-58; S. L. Mead and G. A. Rekers, "The Role of the Father in Normal Psychosexual Development," *Psychological Reports* 45 (1979): 923-31; J. Z. Rubin, F. J. Povenzano, and Z. Luria, "The Eye of the Beholder: Parents' Views on Sex of Newborns," *American Journal of Orthopsychiatry* 44 (1974): 512-19.
4. H. A. Biller, "The Father and Personality Development: Paternal Deprivation and Sex-Role Development," in M. E. Lamb, ed., *The Role of the Father in Child Development* (New York: Wiley, 1976), pp. 89-156; Mead and Rekers; G. A. Rekers, S. L. Mead, A. C. Rosen, and S. L. Brigham, "Family Correlates of Male Childhood Gender Disturbance," *Journal of Genetic Psychology* (in press, 1982); A. C. Rosen and J. Teague, "Case Studies in Development of Masculinity and Femininity in Male Children," *Psychological Reports* 34 (1974): 971-83.
5. See, e.g., A. P. Bell and M. S. Weinberg; and E. Hooker, "Parental Relations and Male Homosexuality in Patient and Non-Patient Samples," *Journal of Consulting and Clinical Psychology* 33 (1969): 140-42.
6. I. Bieber, et. al., *Homosexuality: A Psychoanalytic Study* (New York: Basic Books, 1962).
7. R. B. Evans, "Childhood Parental Relationships of Homosexual Men," *Journal of Consulting and Clinical Psychology* 33 (1969): 129-35; E. Hooker, "Male Homosexuality in the Rorschach," *Journal of Projective Techniques*, 22 (1958), 33-53; E. Hooker, "What Is a Criterion?" *Journal of Projective Techniques* 23 (1959): 278-81.
8. L. B. Apperson and W. G. McAdoo, "Parental Factors in the Childhood of Homosexuals," *Journal of Abnormal Psychology* 73 (1968): 201-6; E. Bene, "On the Genesis of Male Homosexuality: An Attempt at Clarifying the Role of the Parents," *British Journal of Psychiatry* 111 (1965): 803-13.
9. D. G. Brown, "Homosexuality and Family Dynamics," *Bulletin of the Menninger Clinic* 27 (1963): 227-32.
10. Evans, pp. 129-35.
11. Ibid. See also J. Nash and F. Hayes, "The Parental Relationships of Male Homosexuals: Some Theoretical Issues and a Pilot Study," *Australian Journal of Psychology* 17 (1965): 35-43.
12. I. Bieber, et al.

13. M. T. Saghir and E. Robins, *Male and Female Homosexuality: A Comprehensive Investigation* (Baltimore: Williams & Wilkins, 1973).
14. Ibid.
15. Evans, pp. 129-35. See also W. G. Stephan, "Parental Relationships and Early Social Experience of Activist Male Homosexuals and Male Heterosexuals," *Journal of Abnormal Psychology* 82 (1973): 506-13; and Gilbert D. Nass, Roger W. Libby, and Mary Pat Fisher, *Sexual Choices: An Introduction to Human Sexuality* (Monterey, Calif.: Wadsworth, 1981), chap. 15, p. 505.
16. In addition to the studies reviewed above, a number of other psychological and psychiatric investigations provide support for this conclusion. See, e.g., R. Green, *Sexual Identity Conflict in Children and Adults* (New York: Basic Books, 1974); E. M. Hetherington and J. L. Deur, "The Effects of Father Absence on Child Development," *Young Children* 26 (1971): 233-48; B. D. Hore, M. Phil, F. V. Nicolle, B. Chir, and J. S. Calnan, "Male Transsexualism: Two Cases in a Single Family," *Archives of Sexual Behavior* 2 (1973): 317-21; W. McCord, J. McCord, and P. Verden, "Family Relationship and Sexual Deviance in Lower-Class Adolescents," *International Journal of Social Psychiatry* 8 (1962): 165-79; L. E. Newman, "Transsexualism in Adolescence: Problems in Evaluation and Treatment," *Archives of General Psychiatry* 23 (1970): 112-21; A. C. Rosen, G. A. Rekers, and L. R. Friar, "Theoretical and Diagnostic Issues in Child Gender Disturbances," *Journal of Sex Research* 13 (1977): 89-103; R. J. Stoller, "Parental Influences in Male Transsexualism," in R. Green, and J. Money, eds., *Transsexualism and Sex Reassignment* (Baltimore: Johns Hopkins, 1969), pp. 153-69; R. J. Stoller and H. J. Baker, "Two Male Transsexuals in One Family," *Archives of Sexual Behavior* 2 (1973): 323-28; J. Walinder, *Transsexualism: A Study of Forty-three Cases* (Copenhagen: Scandinavian U., 1967); B. Zuger, "The Role of Familial Factors in Persistent Effeminate Behavior in Boys," *American Journal of Psychiatry* 126 (1970): 1167-70.
17. Bell and Weinberg.
18. Ibid.
19. Alan P. Bell, "Research in Homosexuality: Back to the Drawing Board," *Archives of Sexual Behavior* 4, 4 (1975): 421-31.

5

Protecting Your Child's Future

All parents can follow some general guidelines to foster normal sexual development in their children. These guidelines are useful whether or not one's child has ever experienced any homosexual temptation.

HARMONY AT HOME

ESTABLISH A GOOD ENVIRONMENT

From birth, a child needs to receive love from both parents. The newborn child needs cuddling, talking to, and other signs of affection each day. A loving parent-child relationship forms the foundation for a normal heterosexual marriage in the adult years.

Research shows that boys with emotionally distant fathers are prime candidates for homosexual temptation. Many teenage boys who have never felt warmth and acceptance from their fathers later seek out a male with whom to be intimate, trying to make up for the loss of closeness with their fathers. They may not even realize what they are really seeking by pursuing sexual intimacy with another male. A father can largely prevent homosexual temptation for his son if he establishes a long-term affectionate relationship with him from infancy through adolescence. If the father accepts the boy's masculinity in this way, the boy is more likely to accept his own masculinity and will have his emotional needs for closeness to his father fulfilled.

It is more important in a family to engage in activities that encourage positive father-son relationships and mother-daughter relationships. For example, participation in any of the various Christian boys' service organizations is a healthy activity for a boy and his father and provides the opportunity for the father to become a positive role model. Fathers can also spend time playing ball and teaching their sons basic athletic skills, praising them for their accomplishments rather than criticizing their shortcomings. Similarly, mothers and daughters can participate in activities that allow the mother to be a good model of female identity and femininity for the young girl.

It is particularly important that the father be involved in family decision making and in family activities and provide leadership in family life. A father needs not only to have a dominant role in the family but also to be warm, affectionate, and nurturing with both his sons and daughters in order to help them develop a normal sexual identity.[1] A boy learns to respond with love and affection toward women by identifying with his father and observing his father's affection for his mother.

In addition, it is best for the mother to be supportive of the father's leadership in the home and for her to have warm, affectionate relationships with both her sons and her daughters.[2] A girl learns to be affectionate toward men by observing and identifying with her mother.

74

PROVIDE ROLE MODELS

A secure and normal sexual identity in a child is best fostered by a stable home where both father and mother provide affection, attention, and security for their children. If there is a death, separation, or divorce, the number of changes in role models should be as few as possible, for continuity's sake. If the same-sex parent is unavailable for the child, one should attempt to find an appropriate substitute. For example, if the father is not available, a grandfather, older brother, uncle, friend of the family, or someone from a "big brother" program could be enlisted to develop a good relationship with the young boy. A mother can override much of the disadvantage of an absent father if she is able to communicate a positive attitude toward men to the boy, if she finds substitute father figures for the boy to relate to, and if she treats the boy as a male, with a role different from her own.[3] Similarly, a girl would benefit from having a big sister, a grandmother, an aunt, or some other positive female figure to identify with if there is no mother in the home.

A boy needs to learn to accept his masculinity by being accepted as a male by other males. He also learns masculine traits from modeling after men. Similarly, a girl accepts her femininity by being accepted as a female by women, who also provide role models for femininity. Here is a situation in which church members can minister to one another, by providing good role models for children in the Christian community who lack a mother or a father at home.

BE PERCEPTIVE

Parents should realize that young children will normally explore various sex-role behaviors, so it is not unusual, for instance, for a boy to try on a girl's dress or to try out the role of mommy. Parents should not become concerned about this unless it becomes a habit. If a boy does develop excessive feminine behavior, or if a girl develops excessive masculine behavior, the parent should not react anxiously or critically but should try to ignore that behavior and steer the child into appropriate sex-role behavior. Rewarding the child with tokens or points for performing appropriate sex-role behavior, especially behavior the child was avoiding, is more effective than nagging, criticizing, or punishing.[4]

If a child's trying out of opposite sexual roles becomes a persistent pattern, he may be developing a sexual identity problem.[5] Such a child may experience homosexual temptations in his teen and adult years if he does not receive early psychological treatment.[6]

A mother once brought her four-year-old son to see me. This little boy pretended that he was the mother virtually every time he played house.[7] If such a boy rejects his rightful male role, he may also reject the father role, including the idea that he will grow up and marry a woman. So a child's sexual identity problem can be a factor that leads to homosexual or other abnormal sexual temptations later in childhood or adolescence.[8] Adult male homosexuals (both the masculine and feminine types) usually report feminine preferences during much of their childhood.[9]

BE INFORMATIVE

Sometimes a child will have a problem with sexual behavior itself rather than with the sex-role behavior we have been discussing. In this case, a parent needs to be alert and wise in terms of handling that sexual behavior problem itself. For example, if a child plays with himself or herself sexually, the parent can explain that people do not like to see children playing with themselves and that he or she should not be seen doing that.

Then the parent can guide the child to be involved in a different activity or game.[10]

Young children should be discouraged from playing "doctor and nurse" with each other's nude bodies, but they should not be severely reprimanded or punished for that kind of exploratory play. Instead, parents should use the occasion to provide realistic sex education to the child. Sex education books at the child's level can be found in many libraries.

It is important for parents to provide realistic and biblically sound sex education for their child. Young children need to learn the differences between male and female anatomy, and need to learn to accept and appreciate their own anatomies. They also need to learn that all sexual relations should be reserved for marriage.

WHAT'S IN A NAME?

You will recall that because of activities initiated by his father, eight-year-old Danny had become preoccupied with homosexual activities and occasionally tried them out with other children. I discussed with Danny's adoptive mother the fact that Danny's interpretation of his rejection and abuse in the past would be as important as the experiences themselves. If Danny internalizes his previous mental and physical abuse and thinks that it reflects on his somehow being less worthy than other children, he will probably develop a low self-image. If, on the other hand, he can learn that his previous abuse had more to do with his father's having had a problem he will be less likely to feel he deserved the abuse.

In the same way, the interpretation that Danny puts on his own present sexual interest and history of abuse would be important. Young children at school often call each other such names as "gay" and "queer." Sometimes children will even take on a label like that for themselves. If the children with whom Danny was playing were to learn of his homosexual experiences, they might call him a "queer." The main danger for Danny here is that he might in fact take on that label himself.

Many children who have had homosexual experiences imposed upon them mistakenly believe that they really *are* homosexual and are doomed to grow up that way. They think the reason someone imposed homosexual behavior on them was that they were recognized as homosexual, not that the other person had a problem. We know from research that thousands of children who have homosexual experiences imposed upon them grow up to be normal heterosexuals anyway. The difference seems to lie in the child's view of himself or herself. If a child labels himself as gay, it may become a self-fulfilling prophecy.

If a child ever starts giving himself a label like "queer" or "homosexual," the parents should immediately correct him by telling him that the words *homosexual* and *queer* do not even apply to children. They are words for adults. There is no such thing as a homosexual child. The child needs to understand that children are sometimes unkind and give each other untrue labels, but there is no reason to agree with the label.

Preparing for the Future

I also pointed out to Danny's mother that because sexual arousal patterns are not developed in children before puberty, it is possible for them to become sexually aroused through all kinds of events. What is most important is their more general social, psychological, and emotional adjustment. It is a good sign that Danny talks about getting married.

Children at age five or six already understand enough about marriage to know that there are three basic requirements for a marriage partner: (1) the partner must be a person of the opposite sex, (2) the partner must be someone outside one's immediate family, and (3) the partner is usually someone near one's own age.

Young children often think about getting married, and what kind of house they are going to live in, and what kind of car they might drive. They sometimes act out married roles. Playacting and imagining married life is a normal part of growing up[11] and is more important for the child's future sexual adjustment than some sexual experiences they may have had, unless those experiences lead them to label themselves as deviant.

It is important for parents to encourage children in such playacting and imagining. One should be concerned about a child who chronically rejects the idea of growing up to have a family or the idea of ever being married. In all of this, it is essential for the mother and father to provide a good example of married love and commitment to family life. Providing this good example is actually part of good sex education in the home.

It is important for the boy to develop safe, close, warm relationships with boys his age as well as with his father. He should also develop appropriate social relationships with girls his age and with his mother. Some adult men are repulsed by the idea of relating to a woman at all. If a boy develops difficulties in relating normally to girls and women, it might predispose him more to homosexual temptations in adulthood than would isolated homosexual experiences in childhood.

I recommended to Danny's mother that she set up an environment in which he would not be tempted to carry out sexual behavior with other boys. For example, he should not sleep in the same bed with another boy, and, in fact, should have a separate bedroom if possible. I also recommended that he not take baths with his brother. I also recommended that his adoptive father establish an affectionate relationship with Danny to give him an appropriate role model of a loving and caring father.

Danny's new home was an excellent one in which to build his self-esteem. His fears and anxieties had already begun to subside. Although there was evidence of a bit more preoccupation with sexual activity than normal for his age, there was no evidence of a major sexual identity conflict; he was identifying as a male and learning appropriate male roles.

SPIRITUAL RESOURCES

Danny's adoptive parents were Christians, and they had also become Danny's spiritual parents by leading him to an understanding of how to have a right relationship with God. They understood the basic spiritual issues involved in helping Danny overcome sinful temptations and were teaching him to pray to overcome them, as Jesus taught in His model prayer and by direct instruction:

> And do not lead us into temptation, but deliver us from evil [Matthew 6:13].
>
> Keep watching and praying, that you may not enter into temptation; the spirit is willing, but the flesh is weak [Matthew 26:41; see also Mark 14:38; Luke 22:40, 46].

GAY INTERFERENCE

CAN HOMOSEXUALITY BE NATURAL?

From professional experience, I have learned that there are many homosexual activists who would argue against the parents' right to work toward insuring a normal heterosexual adjustment for their children. If parents are not committed to preventing homosexuality in their children, they might give gay liberationists a chance to confuse their offspring.

Should your child's sexual adjustment be left to develop "naturally," as gay liberationists suggest? Letting a child develop along natural lines is relevant only in areas where there are some real biological or temperamental differences among children that should be honored. For example, a child who lacks physical motor coordination should not be forced to become a football star. He should be encouraged to develop some basic athletic skills and to participate in physical education classes in school, but the parent should not force him to be an athlete. In the same way, children have different visual and auditory perceptual abilities. A child who is interested and successful in art and music should not be discouraged if he has a natural visual or auditory talent.

But in the area of sexual adjustment, there is no such thing as a natural development that is not influenced by family, friends, and school personnel. There is no such thing as a "natural" inclination toward homosexual involvement. Instead, there are adverse situations in a child's life that can lead to homosexual temptations. Therefore, responsible parents and clinicians must judge whether the influences on the child are harmful, neutral, or positive.

Sometimes the child's environment is unfortunately biased against his future heterosexual adjustment. Sometimes it happens without the parents' even being aware of negative influences upon the child. But when possible, parents and professionals should be alert to negative influences and should try to rectify them in order to influence the child toward heterosexuality.

Parents should do everything in their power to prevent homosexual temptation from occurring in the first place, and should help the child to resist any homosexual temptation that might occur in spite of their efforts.

In the area of sexuality, all children with healthy bodies have the biological endowment that can lead them to natural adjustment as a heterosexual married partner. It is *natural* for a male to relate biologically to a female. It is *unnatural* for a male to relate sexually to another male. Sexual deviance is never a natural course in a child's development.

THE GAY COUNSELING FRAUD

Some sexual liberationists have suggested that the purpose of psychological therapy is to make an individual more comfortable in his ways. Some misguided psychologists and psychiatrists have proposed that the only appropriate goal of psychotherapy with a person uncomfortable with heterosexuality is for him to be an effective homosexual.

Some even go so far as to recommend that referral to a gay counseling center is the most appropriate option.[12] They say that the only help a child who has a sexual identity problem needs is contact with other individuals like himself. That recommendation is irresponsible and unacceptable.

To refer a child or a teenager to a gay counseling center will seriously interfere with that child's capacity for choice in the future. Such a referral unjustly narrows the person's options to one deviant life-style, because the gay counseling center will encourage a child or teenager to give up the goal of fulfillment through heterosexual marriage in favor of homosexual deviance.[13] Gay counseling centers encourage a destructive life-style that will interfere with personal psychological well-being.

Anyone who refers a child or teenager to a gay counseling center is also guilty of labeling the child, which has potentially disastrous consequences.

Only One Ethical Option

The only appropriate choice in dealing with a child with sexual role problems is to offer psychological treatment at the earliest age. Once parents and professionals have concluded that a child has a sexual role problem, it is unethical not to help the child become normal.[14] It is imperative to help children whose present and future lives are filled with hardship and deviance. With all that is now known about helping children with sexual problems, it is essential that we apply our knowledge to the lives of children and teenagers so that they will not have to struggle with the problems of homosexuality as adults.

Who should have the right to teach children sexual values—homosexual activists or the children's own parents? We should not be intimidated by gay rights activists. The only legitimate goal for parents is for their children to grow up to have a happy, heterosexual family adjustment. To the extent that we can eliminate the temptations toward sexual deviance for our children, we have taken major steps to increase their potential for happy, rewarding, and moral lives that please God.

What is your child's sexual future? Will it be homosexual suffering or family fulfillment? The answer does not depend completely upon the parents, since that child has a free will. A child can rebel against the best moral training. It is the parents' duty, however, to do all they can to eliminate the possibility of homosexual temptations for their child by being alert to early warning signs and by providing a family environment conducive to a normal sexual identity for the child. And if a child has a sexual identity problem, the concerned parent can engage the professional help of a qualified counselor or child psychotherapist (see chapter 8).

1. See Shasta L. Mead and George A. Rekers, "The Role of the Father in Normal Psychosexual Development," *Psychological Reports* 45 (1979): 923-31, for a review of the academic studies reporting this finding.
2. Ibid.
3. Ibid.
4. G. A. Rekers, "Assessment and Treatment of Childhood Gender Problems," in B. B. Lahey and A. E. Kazdin, eds., *Advances in Clinical Child Psychology*, Vol. 1 (New York: Plenum, 1977), pp. 267-306.
5. G. A. Rekers, "Sexual Problems: Behavior Modification," in B. B. Wolman, ed., *Handbook of Treatment of Mental Disorders in Childhood and Adolescence* (Englewood Cliffs, N.J.: Prentice-Hall, 1978) pp. 268-96; G. A. Rekers, "Stimulus Control over Sex-Typed Play in Cross-Gender Identified Boys," *Journal of Experimental Child Psychology* 20 (1975): 136-48; A. C. Rosen and G. A. Rekers, "Toward a Taxonomic Framework for Variables of Sex and Gender," *Genetic Psychology Monographs* 102 (1980): 191-218; P. M. Bentler, G. A. Rekers, and A. C. Rosen, "Congruence of Childhood Sex-Role Identity and Behavior Disturbances," *Child: Care, Health, and Development* 5 (1979): 267-84; G. A. Rekers and S. Mead, "Female Sex-Role Deviance: Early Identification and Developmental Intervention," *Journal of Clinical Child Psychology* 9 (1980): 199-203; G. A. Rekers, A. C. Rosen, O. I. Lovaas, and P. M. Bentler, "Sex-Role Stereotypy and Professional Intervention for Childhood Gender Disturbances," *Professional Psychology* 9 (1978): 127-36.
6. G. A. Rekers, "Therapies Dealing with the Child's Sexual Difficulties," in Jean-Marc Samson, ed., *Enfance et Sexualite/Childhood and Sexuality* (Montreal and Paris: Editions Etudes Vivantes, 1980); G. A. Rekers, "Play Therapy with Cross-Gender Identified Boys," in Charles E. Schaeffer and Kevin J. O'Connor, eds., *Handbook of Play Therapy* (New York: Wiley, forthcoming); G. A. Rekers, O. I. Lovaas, and B. P. Low, "The Behavioral Treatment of a 'Transsexual' Preadolescent Boy," *Journal of Abnormal Child Psychology* 2 (1974): 99-116; G. A. Rekers, C. E. Yates, T. J. Willis, A. C. Rosen, and M. Taubman, "Childhood Gender Identity Change: Operant Control over Sex-Typed Play and Mannerisms," *Journal of Behavior Therapy and Experimental Psychiatry* 7 (1976): 51-57; G. A. Rekers and J. W. Varni, "Self-Monitoring and Self-Reinforcement Processes in a Pre-Transsexual Boy," *Behavior Research and Therapy* 15 (1977): 177-80; G. A. Rekers and J. W. Varni, "Self-Regulation of Gender-Role Behaviors: A Case Study," *Journal of Behavior Therapy and Experimental Psychiatry* 8 (1977): 427-32; G. A. Rekers, T. J. Willis, C. E. Yates, A. C. Rosen, and B. P. Low, "Assessment of Childhood Gender Behavior Change," *Journal of Child Psychology and Psychiatry* 18 (1977): 53-65; G. A. Rekers, "A Priori Values and Research on Homosexuality," *Ameri-*

can *Psychologist* 33 (1978): 510-12; A. C. Rosen, G. A. Rekers, and P. M. Bentler, "Ethical Issues in the Treatment of Children," *Journal of Social Issues* 34 (1978): 122-36.

7. G. A. Rekers and O. I. Lovaas, "Behavioral Treatment of Deviant Sex-Role Behaviors in a Male Child," *Journal of Applied Behavior Analysis* 7 (1974): 173-90.

8. G. A. Rekers, "Pathological Sex-Role Development in Boys: Behavioral Treatment and Assessment" (Ph.D. diss., University of California, Los Angeles, 1972); Rekers, in Lahey and Kazdin; G. A. Rekers, "Psychosexual and Gender Problems," in E. J. Mash and L. G. Terdal, eds., *Behavioral Assessment of Childhood Disorders* (New York: Guilford, 1981); G. A. Rekers, "Atypical Gender Development and Psychosocial Adjustment," *Journal of Applied Behavior Analysis* 10 (1977): 559-71; G. A. Rekers, P. M. Bentler, A. C. Rosen, and O. I. Lovaas, "Child Gender Disturbances: A Clinical Rationale for Intervention," *Psychotherapy: Theory, Research, and Practice* 14 (1977): 2-11; A. C. Rosen, G. A. Rekers, and L. R. Friar, "Theoretical and Diagnostic Issues in Child Gender Disturbances," *Journal of Sex Research* 13 (1977): 89-103; Rekers, Rosen, Lovaas, and Bentler; G. A. Rekers and G. C. Milner, "Sexual Identity Disorders in Childhood and Adolescence," *Journal of the Florida Medical Association* 65 (1978): 962-64; G. A. Rekers and G. C. Milner, "How to Diagnose and Manage Childhood Sexual Disorders," *Behavioral Medicine* 6 (1979): 18-21; G. A. Rekers and G. C. Milner, "Early Detection of Sexual Identity Disorder," *Medical Aspects of Human Sexuality* 15 (1981): 32EE-32FF; G. A. Rekers, "Childhood Identity Disorders," *Medical Aspects of Human Sexuality* 15 (1981): 141-42; H. Bakwin, "Deviant Gender-Role Behavior in Children: Relation to Homosexuality," *Pediatrics* 41 (1968): 620-29; R. Green, *Sexual Identity Conflict in Children and Adults* (New York: Basic Books, 1974); R. Green, "Childhood Cross-Gender Behavior and Subsequent Sexual Preference," *American Journal of Psychiatry* 136 (1979): 106-8; P. S. Lebovitz, "Feminine Behavior in Boys: Aspects of Its Outcome," *American Journal of Psychiatry* 128 (1972): 1283-89; J. Money and A. Russo, "Establishment of Homosexual Gender Identity/Role: Longitudinal Followup of Discordant Gender Identity/Role in Childhood." (Paper Presented at the Meeting of the American Psychological Association, Toronto, Ontario, Canada, August 28—September 1, 1978); B. Zuger, "Effeminate Behavior Present in Boys from Early Childhood: I. The Clinical Syndrome and Follow-up Studies," *Journal of Pediatrics* 69 (1966): 1098-1107.

9. F. L. Whitam, "Childhood Indicators of Male Homosexuality," *Archives of Sexual Behavior* 6 (1977): 89-96; B. Zuger, "Effeminate Behavior Present in Boys from Childhood: Ten Additional Years of Follow-up," *Comprehensive Psychiatry* 19 (1978): 363-69; Rekers, Bentler, Rosen, and Lovaas.

10. L. N. Ferguson and G. A. Rekers, "Non-Aversive Intervention for Public Childhood Masturbation," *Journal of Sex Research* 15 (1979): 213-23.

11. C. B. Broderick, "Normal Sociosexual Development," in C. B. Broderick and Jessie Bernard, eds., *The Individual, Sex, and Society* (Baltimore: Johns Hopkins, 1969) pp. 23-39; C. B. Broderick, "Children's Romances," *Sexual Behavior*, May 1972, pp. 16-21; C. B. Broderick and S. E. Fowler, "New Patterns of Relationships Between the Sexes Among Preadolescents," *Marriage and Family Living* 23 (1961): 27-30; C. B. Broderick and

G. P. Rower, "A Scale of Preadolescent Heterosexual Development," *Journal of Marriage and the Family* 30 (1968): 97-101; S. Millar, *The Psychology of Play* (New York: Aronson, 1974).
12. A. Russell and R. C. Winkler, "Evaluation of Assertive Training and Homosexual Guidance Service Groups Designed to Improve Homosexual Functioning," *Journal of Consulting and Clinical Psychology* 45 (1977): 549-52.
13. For a more detailed analysis of the proper intervention for children, see A. C. Rosen, G. A. Rekers, and P. M. Bentler, "Ethical Issues in the Treatment of Children," *Journal of Social Issues* 34 (1978): 122-36; G. A. Rekers, "Atypical Gender Development and Psychosocial Adjustment," *Journal of Applied Behavior Analysis* 10 (1977): 559-71.
14. Rekers, Bentler, Rosen, and Lovaas.

6

What Young People Should Know About Homosexual Temptations

The sound of thunder and the flashes of lightning punctuated the steady patter of rainfall against the window pane as Debby and Karen looked out at the gray, wet trees in the front yard. Fifteen-year-old Debby had walked over to Karen's rented house near the university before the storm began. The first unexpected flash of lightning and crash of thunder seemed so close that Debby's startled reaction was to grab Karen's knee in fright. Karen comforted Debby with a warm embrace. A rush of emotion welled up in Debby, and her heart began to pound. She tightened her hold on Karen in return. She wondered, *Does Karen know how much this means to me? Does Karen really love me as much as I love her?*

That morning, Debby's mother had discovered and read Debby's diary, which included numerous entries describing her affection for and homosexual experiences with a teenage friend, Sandy, six months earlier. Debby had written about her sexual curiosity, which had led to some sexual experimentation with Sandy. At first Debby had thought of Sandy as just a friend, but after several weeks of sexual play with Sandy, Debby began to write of new romantic feelings toward Sandy. The diary went on to describe Debby's crushed emotions when Sandy severed their relationship, explaining that she could not handle the guilt and the reminder of their sexual experiences when they saw each other, even as friends. Debby described weeks of nights when she cried herself to sleep after that.

Then, after school one day, another schoolmate introduced Debby to twenty-year-old Karen. Karen was outspoken about her involvement in the Gay Student Alliance at the university. Debby's curiosity led to her secret attendance at a few of the Gay Student Alliance meetings, where she became better acquainted with Karen, and Karen had invited Debby over to her house on several occasions. Debby's diary told of her crush on Karen and her quandary over whether to tell Karen how much she desired an intimate relationship with her.

Debby had also written about her confused feelings and thoughts about sexuality. "Karen says that it's foolish to worry about how to change from being a lesbian if you are born that way. Was I born this way? Could I ever fall in love this strongly with a man and get married some day? I'd like to have children. But did God make me gay as Karen says? Does that mean that God made me not to have children? Who is right, Karen or our church minister? He says that sexual relationships were designed by God only for marriage. He says that any other urge for sex is a temptation to sin. Is God tempting me, or what? I'm so confused. But how could I ever ask Mom or Dad for the answer? They would be so shocked. I can't ask them. So what should I do?"

Unfortunately, Debby's mother had been so overwhelmed with anger, guilt, panic, and disgust over what she had read in Debby's diary that she was not calm enough to discuss Debby's concerns with her. Instead, when Debby had arrived home from school, she had confronted Debby with a burst of hostility, accusing her of gross sexual sin and immorality, and insisting that Debby was well on the way to ruining the entire family's reputation. Debby had countered by accusing her mother of violating her right to keep a private diary. The conflict escalated. "How could you do this to me?" was a theme reiterated by both mother and daughter. Finally, Debby had run out of the house in tears and had dashed straight to Karen's house for comfort and sympathy.

The thunderstorm outside was nothing compared to the storm in the hearts of mother and daughter. Unfortunately, Debby's mother had precipitated a crisis in her relationship with Debby instead of answering her questions about sexual temptations. Now in the arms of Karen, Debby was in a situation where she needed to be prepared with a proper understanding of sexual responsibility and temptation. But she had not been taught what she needed to know.

THE ORIGINS OF TEMPTATION

Where do temptations come from? Every parent needs to be able to answer that question, because every child needs to learn about his impulses to evil.

Does God entice people to sin? "Let no one say when he is tempted, 'I am being tempted by God'; for God cannot be tempted by evil, and He Himself does not tempt anyone. But each one is tempted when he is carried away and enticed by his own lust. Then when lust has conceived, it gives birth to sin" (James 1:13-15a).

God is not to be blamed for temptation. Instead, part of the responsibility for temptation to sin lies directly with the individual, who is lured by his own desires.

The Bible also teaches that enticement to do evil may

sometimes come from the devil and that the individual is responsible to resist such temptations originating from outside himself.

> Humble yourselves, therefore, under the mighty hand of God, that He may exalt you at the proper time, casting all your anxiety upon Him, because He cares for you. Be of sober spirit, be on the alert. Your adversary, the devil, prowls about like a roaring lion, seeking someone to devour. But resist him, firm in your faith, knowing that the same experiences of suffering are being accomplished by your brethren who are in the world. And after you have suffered for a little while, the God of all grace, who called you to His eternal glory in Christ, will Himself perfect, confirm, strengthen and establish you [1 Peter 5:6-10].

Although the Bible teaches that there are evil spiritual beings who can tempt us to sin, it also reveals powerful spiritual resources available to each of us to combat those outside influences. So not only are we responsible to resist outside temptations, but we are also provided the means to do so.

> Finally, be strong in the Lord, and in the strength of His might. Put on the full armor of God, that you may be able to stand firm against the schemes of the devil. For our struggle is not against flesh and blood, but against the rulers, against the powers, against the world forces of this darkness, against the spiritual forces of wickedness in the heavenly places. Therefore, take up the full armor of God, that you may be able to resist in the evil day, and having done everything, to stand firm. Stand firm therefore, HAVING GIRDED YOUR LOINS WITH TRUTH, AND HAVING PUT ON THE BREASTPLATE OF RIGHTEOUSNESS, AND HAVING SHOD YOUR FEET WITH THE PREPARATION OF THE GOSPEL OF PEACE; in addition to all, taking up the shield of faith with which you will be able to extinguish all the flaming missiles of the evil one. And take the HELMET OF SALVATION, and the sword of the Spirit, which is the word of God. With all prayer and petition pray at all times in the Spirit, and with this in view, be on

the alert with all perseverance and petition for all the saints [Ephesians 6:10-18].

We are taught to "be on the alert." We need to be aware, as parents, of our children's struggles against their own wrong desires and their struggles against forces in this world that tempt them to homosexual sin. Where do children's desires for homosexual involvements come from? What are the factors in their world that can lead to homosexual temptation? How can they be equipped to resist enticements to homosexuality?

THE CHILD'S WORLD

Homosexual temptations may have many different origins. Some children, like Danny, had homosexual behavior imposed on them in early childhood. That can result in homosexual thoughts remaining in the memory that, when recalled, may later result in homosexual temptation.

For others, like Debby, sexual curiosity leads to sexual experimentation with a member of the same sex. Once such an experience or set of experiences has occurred, they are stored in memory and, when recalled, may tempt the person to repeat the homosexual behavior.

Other children accidentally or otherwise observe homosexual behavior in other children or adults. Those memories can become homosexual temptations later on.

Some children may see homosexual pornographic magazines or movies. The pictures would be images in their memories that can tempt them to lust or behave in a homosexual manner.

In the absence of proper sex education from a parent, a child might acquire homosexual ideas from any of those sources and then pursue the homosexual thoughts or acts themselves. Without proper sex education, Debby was pursuing homosexual relationships even in the face of many conflicting thoughts and feelings.

CONTROLLING FUTURE TEMPTATION

Once the first homosexual temptation occurs, it can become strengthened or weakened depending on the person's response. That is an important lesson for parents to teach children. If the first homosexual temptations are ignored and not translated into either lust or behavior, subsequent temptations are generally weaker and less difficult to resist. But every time a person gives in to a homosexual temptation, the nervous system's responsiveness to the homosexual stimulus becomes stronger. Thus the next temptation will be a stronger one. By having engaged in homosexual fantasies and behavior, Debby had increased her responsiveness to homosexual temptation.

A passage in the Bible reflects this psychological fact: "Do not be deceived, God is not mocked; for whatever a man sows, this he will also reap. For the one who sows to his own flesh shall from the flesh reap corruption, but the one who sows to the Spirit shall from the Spirit reap eternal life. And let us not lose heart in doing good, for in due time we shall reap if we do not grow weary" (Galatians 6:7-9).

Homosexual temptations operate much like any other kind of temptation. There are people who have never been tempted to smoke cigarettes. They were never influenced to try smoking, they may never have tried it, and in fact what they know about lung disease may make the idea of even trying to smoke repugnant. But other people were either pressured to smoke or started to smoke on their own after observing others do

92

it. Once they practiced smoking, they became used to its initial unpleasantness and grew to enjoy it. Now if they want to quit smoking, they must resist many temptations. Rabbi Akiba is quoted as saying, "At the beginning [sin] is like a thread of a spider's web, but in the end it becomes like a ship's cable."[1]

SELF-CONTROL

Although some events that contribute to vulnerability to homosexual temptation are beyond a person's own control, deliberate personal choice is obviously a major force in directing a person's sexual interest. If a teenager chooses to dwell on homosexual thoughts or seek out homosexual pornography, the appeal of homosexuality will be reinforced and strengthened in his nervous system.

The theory that best fits the available scientific information is that for a homosexual orientation to develop, vulnerability to homosexual temptation must be combined with conscious choices in feeding one's sexual fantasies. Even after homosexual orientation has developed, each instance of homosexual behavior actually requires a conscious, voluntary choice by the person to translate his sexual desire into action. In normal, nonneurotic persons, even dwelling on homosexual fantasies involves a decision not to redirect one's thoughts. Sexual behavior requires both the voluntary (central) and involuntary (autonomic) parts of the nervous system to be working together. A person may not be able to control the involuntary aspect of sexual arousal at a given moment, but he is still in control of the voluntary behavior required for sexual activity. The involuntary nervous system's responsiveness to a homosexual stimulus or thought constitutes temptation. But for temptation to become lust or homosexual behavior requires the participation of the voluntary nervous system, which can be controlled.

We know that many, if not most, people with homosexual temptations express a belief that their earliest curiosity in same-sex physical relations was something not deliberately chosen but something that "happened" to them. However, we must face the fact that approximately one-third of all males have experienced enough curiosity or temptation to engage in at least one instance of homosexual behavior, and yet only 4 percent of adult males retain only homosexual conduct as a predominant pattern for a lifetime.[2]

Similarly, 11 percent of females have been curious enough to perform a homosexual act, and yet only 1 percent persist in exclusively homosexual activity throughout adulthood.[3]

Apparently initial curiosity must be followed by conditioning the nervous system to respond more and more to homosexual stimuli.

SEXUAL RESPONSIBILITY

This consideration of the psychological facts supports a Christian view of sexual responsibility. The Bible's teachings about sexual behavior assume that individuals are morally responsible for their sexual acts[4] (see Exodus 20:14; Leviticus 20:10-21; Deuteronomy 22:22-30; Matthew 19:4-9; Mark 10:6-12; John 8:1-11; 1 Corinthians 5:1-5; 6:9-20; 7:8-16; Jude 7). People can choose to act or not act upon an urge, whether it be an urge to steal, to murder, to lie, or to perform a homosexual act (Galatians 6:7-9; Colossians 3:5; 2 Timothy 2:22; James 1:13-15; 1 Peter 2:11).

This is the point where psychology and theology meet. Psychological research can illuminate the complex pattern of psychological factors that may predispose one sexual preference over another. But the Bible makes it clear that the individual at each moment in life is faced with choices either to drift along the easy way by deciding to act upon an urge, or to exhibit moral integrity by deciding to control one's behavior in obedience to God's command (Exodus 20:1-17; Ephesians 6:10-18; James 4:7-8).

There is no proof in psychological science to support the belief that a person is merely a victim of environmental forces that determine his every action. Total determinism is a philosophical viewpoint taken by faith, not a hypothesis that can be proved.

The knowledge that each person has a choice provides great hope for the person who has been troubled by abnormal sexual conduct. Homosexual behavior need not be practiced. But choice also brings with it the forceful reality of individual sexual responsibility. The same fact that provides hope for the sexual sinner also condemns him when he breaches God's moral law for human sexuality (1 Corinthians 6:9-11).

The clear teaching of Scripture, uncontradicted by psychological research, is that homosexual actions are sinful, but the Bible does not end with condemnation of sin. Instead it promises a way out of every homosexual temptation: "No temptation has overtaken you but such as is common to man; and God is faithful, who will not allow you to be tempted beyond what you are able, but with the temptation will provide the way of escape also, that you may be able to endure it" (1 Corinthians 10:13).

Captivity to homosexual behavior is captivity by choice. Even captivity to homosexual orientation is substantially, if not completely, the psychological accumulation of the conditioning effects of choice upon choice, upon choice.

"Submit therefore to God. Resist the devil and he will flee from you. Draw near to God and He will draw near to you. Cleanse your hands, you sinners; and purify your hearts, you double-minded" (James 4:7-8).

Unfortunately, some teenagers have developed a homosexual orientation by unwilling participation in homosexual activities forced upon them. This leads to a state of activity that was never sought and not chosen. But even in those cases the key to release from captivity is the choice to cease homosexual activity. The conditioning principle of "extinction" can then operate to reduce the strength of the homosexual orientation over time.

I once counseled a fifteen-year-old boy who had been forced to perform homosexual acts from the time he was eleven until he was fourteen. As a result, homosexual actions that had initially been repulsive to him had become pleasurable after a while. Finally he found himself repeatedly tempted to initiate homosexual behavior with other boys his age. I counseled him on how to resist the homosexual temptations he was experiencing, and he chose to follow my advice. Months later, he found that he experienced fewer and fewer homosexual desires, as a result of ceasing all homosexual involvements.

Young people who participate deliberately in a gay life-style must face the facts of their sexual behavior. The gay liberation demand for "freedom of choice" in their sexual practices is closer to reality than is some of their other rhetoric. Indeed, repeated homosexual activity is a choice.

TELLING YOUNG PEOPLE ABOUT SEXUAL TEMPTATIONS

Parents need to teach their children these lessons about sexual temptation and sexual responsibility. This is more important in sex education than teaching all the detailed terminology for male and female anatomy. The themes of this chapter need to be taught and reinforced year by year as the child grows toward the teen years. Children need to know that it is unscientific to conclude that sexual behavior is caused by a biological determinant or that sexual behavior is simply a result of psychological causes beyond the person's control. They need to understand that resisting temptation is not only possible, but necessary as well. Teaching the child that temptation should not be acted upon with lust or homosexual behavior will help the child avoid experiences that would make the temptation even stronger.

What children need to understand *before* their bodies mature into adulthood is this: *sexual relations should be reserved for marriage* (Matthew 15:19; 1 Corinthians 6:9; 7:2).

Sexual happiness in marriage is often ruined because of one partner's past failure to live up to this law of human nature. I have counseled numbers of people who discovered this too late. They wish they could live their lives over again and reserve their sexual relations for marriage only. They suffer all kinds of psychological, social, and spiritual problems because they violated this reality.

Consider, for a moment, the reality of the *law of gravity*. Whether a person knows how gravity works or not, if he tries to defy it by jumping off the roof of a three-story building, he will get hurt. Trying to be a special exception to a physical law results in physical damage.

In the same way, whether or not a person is taught about the law of marriage he can be hurt if he violates it. A sexual relationship outside the protective, loving confines of marriage results in harm to the person; trying to be an exception to the psychological and spiritual law of marriage results in psychological and spiritual damage.

Frank questions about sex are sometimes embarrassing to face. Many parents ignore them altogether and thereby fail to warn their children of the dangers of experimenting with sexual relations before marriage. Let's be different. Let's help our children before they reach their teen years. Let's face their questions head on. Let's be specific about the realities of sexuality and teach our children sexual responsibility.

---

1. Cited in Paul Benjamin, "Temptation," in Carl F. H. Henry, ed., *Baker's Dictionary of Christian Ethics* (Grand Rapids: Baker, 1973), p. 666.
2. A. C. Kinsey, W. B. Pomeroy, and C. E. Martin, *Sexual Behavior in the Human Male* (Philadelphia: Saunders, 1948).
3. A. C. Kinsey, W. B. Pomeroy, and C. E. Martin, *Sexual Behavior in the Human Female* (Philadelphia: Saunders, 1953).
4. See Herbert J. Miles, *Sexual Understanding Before Marriage* (Grand Rapids: Zondervan, 1971).

7

Sexual Choices in the Teen Years

"Last Friday, when nobody else was home, I took Mom's sharpest knife out of the kitchen drawer, and I decided that this time I would do it. Really, there's no reason to go on living anymore. Nobody understands how frustrated and unhappy I am."

From all outward appearances, I suppose no one would have guessed that Ken was struggling with such dire conflicts. He was a good-looking teenager of medium athletic build, dressed in blue jeans and a T-shirt. He looked like the typical, all-American boy that might live down the street. But something terrible was bothering him: despair over his homosexual involvements.

Ken had been depressed on other occasions, but this time what was dragging him down was his grief over losing his homosexual lover, who, in addition to physical attention, had lavished Ken with money and gifts.

Ken was more confused, more unhappy, and in much greater trouble than his mother realized when she brought him to my office. She had no idea that Ken had begun seeking out homosexual bars in order to pick up casual sexual partners in the hopes that promiscuous gratification would put him in a better mood. But his recent succession of anonymous homosexual encounters had left him feeling as empty and depressed as before.

Ken had quickly learned that his youth and physical attractiveness placed him in high demand in the gay world. All the social and physical attention he received at the gay bars flattered his ego and boosted his low self-concept. His homosexual encounters did not cure his depression as he had hoped; instead his loneliness and sense of inadequacy made him vulnerable to flattery and exploitation.

At a time when other teenagers are thinking about dating and daydreaming about the possibility of college, future careers, and being married, Ken was daydreaming about finding an older homosexual male who would provide him easy spending money in exchange for sexual favors. He thought he had figured out the easiest way to get by. He felt uneasy about submitting to certain sexual practices, and he had no affection for these older men, but he was gradually overcoming his aversion to the sexual favors required, and he enjoyed the easy money.

During our therapy sessions it became clear to me that it was very important to Ken that I have a Christian outlook on life even though he was not a Christian himself. He sensed that his sexual life-style was violating the moral structure of the universe, and he sensed that he needed spiritual as well as psychological solutions to his dilemmas. But in spite of his internal conflicts, he had decided that the pleasures of the gay lifestyle were something that he did not want to pass up during his teenage years. Although he sensed the moral and personal costs of his decision, he was impressed by the material reward and physical pleasure that his attractiveness could bring him.

Ken continued in individual psychotherapy sessions once a week for two months. I was able to help him overcome much of his severe depression and to help alleviate the intensity of his sexual identity confusion. But when I gave Ken the option to direct his therapy toward the goal of overcoming his homosexual lifestyle, he took a tragically naive approach.

"Later on, maybe in my late twenties, I'd like to fall in love with a woman, get married, and have a happy family with a few kids. By then, I'll completely give up my homosexual affairs, because I'm sure my wife would want me to go to bed only with her.

"I just can't imagine continuing to live my whole life in the gay world. I really want to have kids, and I want to be a better dad to them than my dad was for me. The gay life just doesn't lead to anything. It just doesn't end up with a family."

I agreed that Ken could choose to allow his sexuality to provide him with a normal family life, or he could choose to let it destroy that possibility.

Ken reflected, "I know that when I get older, the gays won't pay as much attention to me anymore."

"Yes," I observed, "older homosexual men have told me that they have to depend almost completely on paying for their sex once they are no longer young and attractive. Their sex life has no connection with personal love and commitment to another's needs. And they've thrown away the chance to have a family with children and grandchildren. It's important for you to look ahead and to consider something more than just the sexual thrill of the moment."

Ken replied, "Well, yes. And I'm worried that God will send me to hell if I live my life as a homosexual. Eventually, I want to straighten up. But I know that when I'm young, my body is more appealing than it ever will be again. What I want is to experience the thrill of the gay life for two years. Then when I'm almost eighteen, I'll straighten up in time to get married when I'm in my twenties. I just don't want to pass up the good times now. Besides, I'm not ready to get married, so I might as well live it up while I can."

For the next three psychotherapy sessions, I tried to help Ken think through the folly of his pursuing a two-year period of homosexual prostitution. Through step-by-step questions, I helped him think through the risks of getting an untreatable form of venereal disease. I led him to an awareness of the risks of encountering violent homosexual men. I let him know how important the later teen years are for conditioning his nervous system to become more responsive to sexual stimuli. I explained that it would be much easier for him to return to normal heterosexuality now, at age fifteen, than if he immersed himself in homosexuality for the next two years.

Ken understood the risks involved in his plan, but unfortunately, he did not fully appreciate the risk that after two years of homosexual prostitution he might not be thinking about heterosexual family fulfillment any more. He decided to quit therapy, and he returned to a busy homosexual life of prostitution and searching for a male lover.

Ken's future is very bleak if he persists in his chosen path. But he can, if he wishes, change his path.

Every teenager faces some basic sexual choices. The parent who has discovered that his teenager has become involved in homosexuality should try lovingly to communicate a message of hope and responsibility to the young person. It is important to build the loving bridge of communication and caring; lashing out with Mosaic denunciations would not be the best first step.

The main points of this book should be openly and

frankly discussed with a teenager: the distinctions between homosexual behavior, lust, and temptation; the difference between friendly affection and homosexuality; the dangers and drawbacks of homosexuality; the myths perpetrated by the gay liberation movement; and especially the moral and spiritual solution to the problem. Ken's case could serve as an instructive example for discussion. It is often easier to be objective when we discuss someone else's situation rather than our own.

It would be of help, as well, for the teenager to consider some concepts about self-control and sex. Self-control has been intensively researched by psychologists over the past ten years,[1] and clinical psychologists have developed many different strategies by which people can control their thoughts, emotions, or actions. These strategies have been successfully used to help people stop bad habits such as smoking, overeating, and negative thinking.

The two main self-control strategies are environmental planning and behavioral programming.

ENVIRONMENTAL PLANNING

Environmental planning includes those strategies that a person can use to make changes in his own environment which, in turn, will influence his behavior. For example, a person can plan and carry out a strategy of keeping himself from ever attending a gay bar, where he would be tempted to take a sexual partner. Or he can change his environment by throwing away any homosexual pornography he may have collected. This would eliminate the possibility that he would come across the pornography and be tempted to read it. In other cases, a person may plan to avoid being alone with anyone who tempts him to have homosexual relations.

There are many types of environmental-planning

strategies that can be used to help gain self-control over homosexual temptations. Choosing the path of sexual purity means choosing to put oneself in wholesome situations.

BEHAVIORAL PROGRAMMING

Behavioral programming strategies involve self-imposed consequences for behavior. Those consequences can be either self-rewards or self-punishments.

For example, if a person who is tempted by homosexual thoughts successfully puts the idea out of mind, he can reward himself with the thought, "I did a good thing by avoiding that temptation." That will strengthen his self-control. Or if he drives by a theater that displays an ad for a homosexual movie, he can keep on driving and reward himself with the thought, "I'm glad I passed up that temptation."

This strategy can also involve more tangible rewards. A person who has been struggling with the temptation to go to homosexual bars could reward himself with a special treat such as a favorite dessert at the end of a week when he has avoided those bars altogether. Or he can reward himself with a new shirt for reaching the goal of avoiding a past homosexual "lover" for a week. Such rewards make it easier to achieve self-control in the future.

Self-punishments such as "thought stopping" can also help self-control. Each time his mind turns to a homosexual thought, he can mentally tell himself, "Stop that!" as a mild punishment. If he is alone in a car or empty room, he might even say it out loud to break the thought sequence in mind. That strategy has helped people overcome other kinds of negative thoughts, and it holds potential for helping a person decrease homosexual lustful thoughts as well.

The most important recommendation for a teenager

trying to cope with homosexual temptations is that he personally respond to God's invitation to obtain moral forgiveness and spiritual rebirth. Once a relationship with God has been established, he or she may benefit from the following recommendations:

Pray regularly for success in resisting any homosexual temptations experienced (Matthew 6:13; 1 Corinthians 10:13). Complete sexual abstinence until marriage is not only possible for each teenager but is also the most normal and beneficial option.[2]

Stay away from anyone or anything such as gay movies, homosexual pornography, gay bars, or homosexual acquaintances that elicit homosexual thought or behavior. Job 28:28 teaches, "Behold, the fear of the Lord, that is wisdom; and to depart from evil is understanding" (italics added). Second Timothy 2:22 instructs us: "Now flee from youthful lusts, and pursue righteousness, faith, love and peace, with those who call on the Lord from a pure heart."

When homosexual thoughts arise, redirect your thinking to pure thoughts about different topics. Philippians 4:8 gives this helpful advice: "Whatever is true, whatever is honorable, whatever is right, whatever is pure, whatever is lovely, whatever is of good repute, if there is any excellence and if anything worthy of praise, let your mind dwell on these things."

Obtain psychotherapy from a Christian therapist for any or all of the following: (a) to distinguish abnormal sexual desires from deep friendship or attachment needs, (b) to develop better insights into one's problems and personality, (c) to help control homosexual urges, (d) to eliminate homosexual temptation through behavior therapy, or (e) to help develop social ease with members of the opposite sex.

Self-control is easier for some than for others, but everyone has a choice regarding sexual lusts and sexual actions. Some people can benefit from better personal planning for self-control, and psychologists have discovered many helpful self-control strategies.

At the outset of chapter 1, I told the story of Kirk, who exercised his power of choice by seeing a Christian clinical psychologist for help in achieving normal married sexual adjustment. He took his responsibility seriously and sought help when he needed it. Kirk is an example of one who exercised responsible self-control. He was not homosexually tempted as strongly as some others are, but whether a temptation is strong or weak, the same principles of choice apply.

A qualified Christian counselor, clinical psychologist, or psychiatrist can assist the responsible individual who is willing to develop the skills of self-control over sexual conduct. The following chapter describes how one can choose a good counselor or therapist.

1. William H. Redd, Albert L. Porterfield, and Barbara L. Andersen, *Behavior Modification: Behavioral Approaches to Human Problems* (New York: Random House, 1979).
2. Frank M. duMas, *Gay Is Not Good* (Nashville: Nelson, 1979), p. 191.

III
Triumph over Homosexuality

8

Help and Hope for Those Already Involved

"I'm coming to talk with you for my parents' sake only," Tammy confessed as she introduced herself to me in her first visit to my office. Tammy was seventeen years old, and her parents had insisted that she see me for psychological help.

Tammy was willing to talk honestly about herself, but she was not certain that she wanted to give up her homosexual relationship with Laura, a college sophomore. Both Tammy and Laura were Christians, and they both believed the Bible's teaching against homosexual practices. But they had been involved in a homosexual relationship for seven months, and neither of them was eager to give it up, even though they felt guilty.

Tammy was experiencing several conflicts because of her homosexual involvement. At home, Tammy felt the tension created since her brother and parents had learned about her affair with Laura. Sometimes the conflict was direct. For example, her dad would often tell her, "Sexual sin is just like smoking—all you have to do is decide to quit, and then quit, cold turkey."

Tammy would complain that he did not understand how difficult quitting would be for her. Other times the conflict at home was indirect, such as when her brother would look at her with exasperation and shake his head in disbelief. Tammy felt a barrier between herself and Andy that she did not know how to handle.

Tammy had made a deep commitment to her Christian faith several years earlier. She realized that her sexual involvement with Laura was inconsistent with her Christian commitment. She reflected, "Usually, I try to put my beliefs about sex completely out of my mind, but I can't avoid thinking about how my beliefs and my life are going in opposite directions. I feel stuck. I can't give up my Christian beliefs, but I can't give up Laura, either." Tammy's guilt over her sexual experiences had led to a growing disinterest in attending the youth group and worship services at church over the past year.

Tammy was distressed over having to be continuously on guard so that people wouldn't find out about her homosexuality. When she and Laura were in a group together, Tammy felt stilted and unnatural; she felt that she couldn't be her "real self." She and Laura also had to sneak around and lie to people in order to arrange times to be alone together. Tammy was beginning to feel more and more uncomfortable about deceiving her friends and family, and she questioned herself for living a double life.

Tammy was also experiencing an identity conflict. "I've always thought of myself eventually getting married and having children. I really want to be a mother someday." But she realized that if she continued her relationship with Laura, she would continue to avoid dating any boy her age. Laura was jealous of any attention that a boy showed toward Tammy. Tammy tried to stay away from getting to know teenage boys so as not to offend Laura. She did not dislike boys, but she wondered if she could ever feel the same intense love for a man that she felt for Laura.

She asked a lot of questions about homosexuality, about the possibility of being happily married someday, and about how other people had learned to cope with the kinds of problems she was experiencing. She expressed deeper and deeper anguish over her predicament. She could not stand the idea of giving up her relationship with Laura, but she could not stand the idea of continuing in her family conflict, her spiritual conflict, her social conflict, and her identity conflict.

I can still recall the day Tammy came in for her seventh session. She had a smile on her face. "Mom said she really noticed a big change in me—for the better. My brother, Andy, said I'm in a better mood now. So yesterday I told them why. Last week I broke up with Laura. I told her that I just couldn't go on with our relationship because it was wrong. She cried, and I cried, but I stuck to it.

"What a relief! It's like a heavy load of guilt has been taken off my back. I've gotten over my rotten, depressed mood, and before I even told anyone what I'd done, so many people commented to me how much different I am now. I never thought it would make that kind of difference.

"Laura and I can still be friends, but I've decided to move away from home to go to college. Laura wanted me to attend the university here in town, but I'll be better off moving away from her, I'm sure. Oh, it still hurts to think I won't see her much anymore, but this is what I have to do."

Tammy was able to chart a course away from homosexual temptation and toward a normal, heterosexual life. She continued in psychotherapy for many months to help in the transition, and she became actively involved in a church near her college, where she found moral support and spiritual nurture.

HELPING OTHERS LIKE TAMMY

If a teenager makes wrong choices in response to homosexual temptation, homosexual lusts or acts may become bad habits. Granted, certain family factors may have predisposed a young person to have strong homosexual temptations. Granted, other youths or adults may have initiated the homosexual practices. Granted, the young person may not have been fully aware of the consequences of repeated homosexual fantasies. But regardless of the origins of the homosexual temptations, young people who yield to them do so by an act of the will. Each instance of dwelling on homosexual lust or of homosexual practices is chosen by the young person, however naive or well informed he or she is.

So a young person like Tammy may develop a homosexual problem. It would be better if all families modeled healthy sexual roles so that psychological pressures toward homosexual temptation would never build up in the first place. It would be better if young people were never sexually initiated into homosexuality by other teens or adults. It would be better if all youth were forewarned to avoid the pitfalls of homosexual fantasy. In short, it would be much better if homosexual temptations could be prevented altogether. But we must often face the challenge of helping a young person like Tammy overcome a homosexual problem that has developed despite our most valiant efforts.

Parents of teenagers troubled by homosexuality should not encourage the problem by letting their youngster decide on his own about his sexual pursuits.

Would a responsible parent let a teenager decide

whether to abuse a dangerous drug? Of course not; it is illegal and destructive to abuse drugs. Would a responsible parent let a teenager decide whether to be a prostitute? Of course not; that too is illegal and destructive.

So should a responsible parent let a teenager decide whether to be involved in homosexual activity? Of course not. Tammy's parents made the right decision when they insisted that she receive psychological help. Homosexual practices are illegal and destructive in terms of breaking sodomy, prostitution, and parental responsibility laws; risking venereal disease; opening oneself up to social rejection; violating basic morality; and damaging one's potential for psychological adjustment and future family fulfillment.

The first step for the parent is to realize that family members are responsible to promote future sexual normality. They must do everything possible to secure the chances of normal sexual development in the children. Parents bear a responsibility to communicate the truth about homosexuality—especially moral and spiritual truths. The foundation for a return to normal sexual fulfillment is the Scriptures' teaching on normality and healthy sexuality.

Parents should take the opportunity to help their teenager by teaching him or her the truths about sexual choices. Future sexual adjustment is not determined by the fates; the teenager can exert self-control in shaping his or her sexual future.

The principles in this book, when properly understood, can help a teenager translate his or her desire for normal, married sexuality into changes that will prepare him or her for future family living.

In addition to teaching, the responsible parent will not allow his teenager to frequent places of homosexual contact.

Not only should parents prevent their teenager from

frequenting such places, but they should also exercise their political power as citizens to insist that the police department enforce the laws against minors being present in them. Teenage boys are at a premium for their youthful sexual attributes, so adult homosexuals running gay establishments often look the other way when teenagers come in.

OUTSIDE HELP

Sometimes the best way to help a teenager with homosexual problems is to obtain professional assistance from a qualified therapist or counselor. The two most common sources of help are clinical psychologists and psychiatrists. The clinical psychologist is a doctor in psychology (Ph.D. or Psy.D.) with nine to twelve years of college, university, and clinical internship or postdoctoral training in behavioral sciences, general psychology, psychological testing, behavioral assessment, psychodiagnosis, psychopathology, abnormal psychology research, individual and group psychotherapy, behavior therapy, and neuropsychology. (The doctor in clinical psychology usually has some training in physiological psychology, psychopharmacology, behavioral medicine, and comparative neuroanatomy as well, but these biological studies are usually supplementary to the main study of mental and emotional disorders, their diagnosis and treatment.)

The psychiatrist is a doctor in medicine (M.D.) who has first spent seven or eight years in college and university education, primarily in the fields of zoology, biology, biochemistry, physiology, surgery, and pharmacology, to receive a degree in general medicine. Then he has typically spent three more years in on-the-job training in psychopharmacology, psychotherapy, neurology, and hospital management of patients.

Both psychiatrists and clinical psychologists diagnose emotional and mental problems and use various psychotherapies to treat people suffering from them. Therefore, psychologists and psychiatrists have many overlapping duties. Clinical psychologists provide a unique service in the in-depth psychodiagnostic assessment made possible by psychological and neuropsychological testing and behavioral assessment. Psychiatrists provide a unique service in prescribing drugs to manage certain types of mental disorders.

The parent or youth seeking professional help must be very cautious in selecting a counselor, because, unfortunately, many psychologists and psychiatrists treat homosexuality and related sexual identity problems apart from a moral framework. Many still view homosexuality as pathological, but they no longer subscribe to the Judeo-Christian principles regarding homosexual conduct.

What is worse, a growing minority of psychologists and psychiatrists argue that it is more appropriate to help a person to adjust to homosexuality rather than to help him change from a homosexual orientation. Some homosexual psychologists have argued that psychotherapists must assist homosexuals to fully accept and value their homosexual identity.[1] (This prohomosexual value position is the approach taken, for example, by the state-funded Center for Homosexual Education, Evaluation, and Research at San Francisco State University.)

So the parent or youth seeking professional assistance needs to be very careful to pick a *qualified* counselor. What qualifies a therapist or counselor to help a teenager with homosexual problems?

1. The counselor should hold the credentials of a mental health profession. If a *psychologist*, the doctor (Ph.D. or Psy.D.) should be state-licensed and, even bet-

ter, should be a Diplomate in Clinical Psychology from the American Board of Professional Psychology. If a *psychiatrist,* the doctor (M.D. or D.O.) should be state-licensed as a physician and have completed a residency program in psychiatry; even better, should be a Diplomate in Psychiatry from the American Board of Psychiatry and Neurology. If a *psychiatric social worker,* the professional (M.S.W. or D.S.W.) should be state-licensed as a clinical social worker and be in the Academy of Certified Social Workers (A.C.S.W.).

2. The professional should have received specific training in human sexuality and sexual problems from a university, hospital, or institute.

3. The professional should view homosexuality as an abnormality (in contrast to the minority of mental health professionals who no longer consider homosexuality undesirable).

4. The professional should have moral values that consider sexual relationships permissible only in the context of legal marriage.

5. The professional should have a vital commitment to the orthodox Christian faith in order to provide spiritual counsel and wisdom as well as psychological help.

WHEN A FULLY QUALIFIED PROFESSIONAL IS UNAVAILABLE

If you are unable to find a therapist or counselor with all of the above qualifications, it is possible to benefit from seeing a professional with qualifications 1 through 4, while simultaneously obtaining spiritual counsel from a pastoral counselor with qualifications 3 through 5.

At the very minimum, you should seek the help of a Christian counselor with qualifications 3 through 5. It would be better to receive spiritually sound counseling in the absence of psychological therapy if your circumstances force a choice between a Christian counselor and a professional therapist lacking qualifications 3 through 5. Tragically, some people have turned to a professional psychotherapist for assistance in overcoming homosexual practices, only to end up with a pro-homosexual psychologist who attempts to talk them out of their own moral choice.

Check on the professional's qualifications over the phone before making an appointment for an office visit. Do not automatically assume that every counselor or therapist calling himself *Christian* is qualified in terms of qualifications 3 through 5. Many so-called Christian counselors and psychotherapists have capitulated to the deception that homosexuality is all right. So check out a counselor before ever seeing him in person.

A responsible counselor or psychotherapist will openly and honestly answer your questions regarding these five qualifications before you schedule a visit. If he refuses to give you straightforward answers in advance of an appointment, you may assume that he is trying to conceal a lack of one or more of the qualifications. Look elsewhere for help. It would be better to receive no therapeutic help at all than to receive the *wrong* kind of professional "help."

WHEN SHOULD PROFESSIONAL HELP BE SOUGHT?

The responsible parent should seek help for his child or teenager at the earliest sign of a sexual identity problem or sexual role problem. It is better to seek help early rather than to delay; it would be much better to find out that a behavior pattern is normal and in no need of treatment than to allow the child to suffer for months or years with an untreated sexual development problem.

The best time to obtain professional help is when a child showing signs of sexual role confusion is young,[2] even as young as four years old. Early involvement in homosexual behavior (as in Danny's case) would also warrant professional consultation.

Some teenagers become aware of a need for help to overcome homosexual temptation and lust even though they have rarely or never succumbed to actual homosexual behavior. They may be succeeding in the moral task of resisting the temptation to translate homosexual urges into action, but they yearn for freedom from the distracting and distressing temptations.

Some teenagers find themselves able to avoid homosexual relationships, but they are plagued with repeated episodes of being tempted to indulge in homosexual lust. They repeatedly entertain homosexual thoughts or look at homosexual pornography. They find their minds drifting into homosexual daydreaming during the school day, when they see attractive same-sex peers in class or in the shower room after gym class. They realize their reactions are not normal, and they worry that their homosexual fantasy life might crowd out normal dating interests and eventually family fulfillment.

Other teenagers may be able to resist homosexual practices and even succeed in resisting homosexual lusts, but they would prefer not being tempted by these menacing distractions. Homosexual temptations make them feel different from their friends, and they would just as soon eliminate the problem in its early stages rather than fight the same battle for years to come.

Such young persons may appropriately seek preventative counseling for themselves. They may want to make sure that they will not give in to a homosexual urge and engage in a homosexual act in some weak moment in the future. Or they may need spiritual or psychological counsel to help control their problem with homosexual lust, if they are otherwise self-controlled in their sexual behavior.

It is best that a teenager or child receive professional help before homosexual temptations result in homosexual activity. But if you sense that your child is already engaged in homosexual practices, that, of course, would also warrant professional help.

So a youngster with homosexual problems might need one or more of several types of help:

1. Help to stop yielding to temptation by engaging in homosexual actions

2. Help to stop yielding to temptation by engaging in homosexual lusts

3. Help to reduce the amount of homosexual temptation

4. Help to overcome the pain of depression, suicidal thoughts, guilt, and low self-image associated with homosexuality

5. Help to take on a normal sex-role socially, and to decrease opposite-sex behavior

6. Help in obtaining sex education in a proper moral framework

7. Help to develop normal dating skills and self-confidence with members of the opposite sex.

If a parent learns that his teenager wants to see a counselor, he should be glad that his son or daughter is open to such assistance. The parent should not pry for details of the teenager's reasons for wanting to see a counselor. Instead, he should devote his energies to insuring that the teenager finds a properly qualified Christian counselor or professional. Once a qualified counselor has been found, the parent should allow the teenager to talk to the counselor in confidence and should let the teenager know that he will not ask the counselor to reveal details of their conversations. That will allow the teenager the freedom to reveal his innermost concerns to the counselor.

Often when children or teenagers first become involved in homosexual practices, they are not aware of the risk they are taking. If they understood the full impact of their homosexual activity, they would be less likely to be involved in it. But youngsters are naive about the dangers of homosexual involvement unless an adult has specifically taught them the importance of proper sexual roles and the proper place of sexuality in married life. Like Tammy, these youngsters may be unaware of all the destructive aspects of homosexual activity, including guilt, shame, public embarrassment, personal health damage, depression, suicidal urges, personal emptiness, emotional hurt from unfulfilled, unrealistic expectations, and social maladjustment.

On the other hand, some children and teenagers do realize that these problems accompany their homosexual activity. They may be keenly aware of the advantages of preparing properly for marriage and family fulfillment in their future. They know that eventually they will have to give up promiscuity in order to be capable of a successful marriage. They may have learned the hard way about the pitfalls and destructiveness of homosexual involvement.

Whether a youth realizes the destructiveness of homosexual activity or not, it is crucial for his parents to obtain the best possible professional and Christian counseling, for themselves and for their youngster. Parents should not delay in this or let their child talk them out of it. They should reason with their child to elicit his or her cooperation in seeking counseling and, if necessary, require it. The problem may involve not only homosexual temptation, lust, and behavior, but also other personal or social difficulties.

Fortunately if the family cooperates with the kind of

spiritual and psychological help available, there is a great likelihood that the homosexual problems can be defeated. A vast number of psychological studies show that the various aspects of the problem with homosexuality can be successfully treated.[3] (Research also indicates that early childhood signs of sexual deviation can also be successfully detected and treated.)[4]

CAN HOMOSEXUALITY REALLY BE HELPED?

Until approximately twenty-five years ago, the general professional consensus was that homosexuality was untreatable — an unfortunate conclusion that resulted, in part, from the mistaken notion that the condition was biologically rooted. Since the establishment of scientific evidence that homosexuality is not biologically determined, there have been many attempts to treat it. Hormonal treatment was found to be ineffective, but long-term individual psychotherapy, psychoanalysis, group psychotherapy, behavior therapy, and aversive conditioning therapy have all been applied with certain degrees of success.

There are different ways to evaluate the research on the treatment of homosexuals. If we consider any significant movement toward heterosexual adjustment as success, studies on the treatment of homosexuality show that, on the average, 50-75 percent of the treated persons improved (improvement rates reported have varied from 30 percent to 100 percent). If one uses a more stringent criterion, which requires that a person become exclusively heterosexual in orientation and behavior after therapy, results of the studies show between 6 percent and 40 percent success. In any case, we can be optimistic about the outcome of psychological treatment for homosexual problems.[5]

Studies show that some types of individuals respond more favorably to psychological treatment than others:

121

those who are young, those with motivation to change, those with conscious guilt about their homosexual behavior, and those for whom the onset of the homosexual problem is recent. Those findings help explain why the Christian view of homosexuality has high therapeutic value. Those who are willing to view their homosexuality as a problem have a better chance of solving their problem. The gospel offers a wonderful opportunity for repenting of homosexuality and provides motivation to change. Significantly, the majority of those motivated to overcome homosexuality have religious or moral reasons for their motivation. Dr. Mansell Pattison, chairman of the psychiatry and health behavior department at the Medical College of Georgia reported eight individuals who overcame their homosexual problems not through psychotherapy but through a Christian ministry to homosexuals. In that setting, as well, change was easier for the younger adults than for the older ones.[6]

Hundreds of individuals have overcome their homosexuality. Wanting to change is the biggest key; then receiving the right kind of help can complete the process.

WHAT KINDS OF HELP ARE AVAILABLE?

There are a number of ways in which a properly qualified Christian counselor or psychotherapist can assist young people troubled by homosexuality.

First of all, the counselor will need to be sensitive to the spiritual condition of the youth. One cannot force a Christian solution to a problem, but the counselor can have wise advice available. The counselor can recommend and join in prayer for success in resisting the temptation toward homosexual lust and behavior (Matthew 6:13; 1 Corinthians 10:13) as well as for freedom from the homosexual urges themselves.

SELF-UNDERSTANDING

Young people can be helped in psychotherapy to distinguish sexual drives from deep friendship needs. You will recall Kirk, who needed help in making the distinction in order to understand his needs better. A desire for same-sex friendships should not be confused with homosexual temptation.

Unresolved emotional needs for closeness or conflicts about sexual roles due to family upbringing can also be dealt with in psychotherapy. Tammy, for example, was helped by gaining insight into her conflicts over homosexuality and facing them squarely instead of suppressing them. Acknowledging conflicts will often reduce the frequency and drive of homosexual urges that are at the root of homosexual temptations.

SELF-CONTROL

It is a psychological truth that one can feel an urge without needing to act upon it. Just because a homosexual urge is experienced, there is no psychological imperative to act on that urge. It is not a psychological "need" that requires fulfilling, and the young person will not be psychologically hurt by refusing to act upon it.

To help a young person achieve better self-control over such urges, a professional can use psychotherapy, behavior therapy, and spiritual counseling. The self-control strategies outlined in the previous chapter can be taught in depth and applied to the everyday circumstances of the young person receiving counseling.

One "environmental planning" strategy is to help the teenager, through diaries, behavior checklists, or interviewing, to discern what places and things elicit homosexual thoughts. Then the professional can help the teenager figure out the most effective ways of staying away from those places, people, or things (cf. Job 28:28; 2 Timothy 2:22).

Various behavior therapy techniques have been developed to reduce or eliminate homosexual responsiveness of the nervous system. Both mildly aversive therapy procedures and nonaversive conditioning techniques can help erase homosexual arousal patterns and substitute normal heterosexual arousal patterns. These therapy techniques can be extremely helpful in eliminating the last traces of homosexual orientation, especially in young people.

Behavior therapies sometimes require that the professional have certain equipment available in his office and specialized training in behavior therapy.[7]

TRAINING IN SOCIAL SKILLS

Over the past decade, a great deal of attention has been given to helping people develop successful dating skills. Many young people, not just those with homosexual problems, are shy, especially around a member of the opposite sex with whom they would like to spend time, and they need help in feeling comfortable in dating situations. Psychotherapists have access to much that has been written on the best ways to help youth be comfortable and skilled in socializing with members of the opposite sex.

FROM THEORY TO PRACTICE

John, the sixteen-year-old boy described in chapter 3, is an example of how one can benefit from psychotherapy. For personal, moral, and social reasons, John was highly motivated to overcome his homosexual involvement. He needed all seven kinds of help outlined above, and he received the elements of successful counseling just described.

Over the course of a year of therapy sessions, John gradually stopped having sexual relations with males and stopped his visits to gay bars. He learned to cease careless talk about his homosexual escapades that only served to label him among his peers. He learned to cease flirting with males and to dress and act in more masculine manners, which improved his self-image and his acceptance with both boys and girls his age. He began to date girls, to enjoy them as girl friends, and to be comfortable in the dating role.

He stopped reading homosexual pornography, and conditioning therapy helped reduce the strength of his homosexual urges. He was able to achieve more self-control over sexual thoughts about males.

John would have preferred an instant cure for his homosexuality, but release was gradual. He learned first how to control his sexual actions, even though he still experienced homosexual temptations. After five or six months of counseling he began to apply successfully the strategies of self-control over lustful fantasies. The process of improvement required a lot of hard work and vigilance on John's part, but as he stopped feeding his mind with homosexual fantasies, his homosexual urges decreased and he was tempted less often.

A major step in John's improvement was his coming to grips with the moral and spiritual dimensions of his sexual problems. That was also a gradual process. He accepted scriptural teachings on sexuality first, and then began to apply them to his own life. He learned to look to the Lord to obtain forgiveness and the strength to resist homosexual temptations.

At the end of the school year, John moved to another town. A year later, he called to tell me how he was doing. He had found new friendships among people who had no knowledge of his prior homosexual involvements. That made it easier to develop a new, normal male role. As his outward role became normal, his self-concept as a normal male was also strengthened.

John was still motivated to please God in his sexual life, and he had prayed for forgiveness on the two occasions when he had given in and engaged in homosexual activity. However, he was not tempted as frequently or as intensely, and he had greatly improved in his control over his sexual conduct when temptations did arise. He was confident that he would continue to improve, and he was pleased that the problems he had lived with for so many years had been substantially overcome after one year of therapy and another year of applying what he had learned through therapy.

John's story is not completed. He is still living, and so he will face sexual choices continually. No one, including John, is completely pure in fantasy and conduct. But John is well on his way toward his goal of being faithful to a married partner and raising a normal family. He has learned how to master his own sexual life by controlling his sexual actions and thoughts, and he has learned how to accept himself in a normal male role. These were the improvements that we had hoped and prayed for.

John, as everyone, will experience sexual temptations of various types from time to time. Sometimes he may be tempted with a homosexual urge and on other occasions he may now be tempted with a heterosexual urge toward a woman who is not his wife. It would be unrealistic for John to expect a total elimination of all impure sexual urges as his evidence of a "cure."

Instead, John may be required to live with occasional sexual urges in directions that he does not morally approve, but he can cope with them by refusing to yield to them in either thought or action. That is what constitutes success.

As John grows from an adolescent to an adult, he should expect to develop greater emotional and spiritual maturity that will enable him to enjoy greater self-control in his sexual life. An occasional failure to resist a sexual temptation is wrong, damaging, and regrettable. But an instance of failure is not a license to give up hope and to abandon oneself to all future sexual urges. Instead, an instance of failure is an occasion to ask God's forgiveness, to strengthen one's resolve for better self-control in the future, and to resist the notion of being hopelessly doomed to abnormal sexuality.

How to Help a Young Person with Homosexual Problems

A parent, teacher, or friend of a young person like John can be a source of encouragement and help. It is important not to act rashly, but to be loving, mature, and wise in guiding that person back to the right track. Disowning a young person with homosexual struggles will not help; it may be uncomfortable to think about the youth's problem, but driving him or her away will not make the problem go away.

How, then, should you respond to a young person who has confided in you about a homosexual problem? Or what should be your reaction to knowledge gained in some other way that a young person has this kind of difficulty?

BE A FRIEND

First and foremost, be a warm and understanding listener. Keep communication lines open with the youth. Let him know that you will pray for and with him. Use the Bible for comfort and assurance (1 Corinthians 6:11). Be a friend to that person, offering help and encouragement for any effort he or she makes to overcome the problem.

Many young people troubled by homosexuality lead lonely and isolated lives. They have felt rejection by many people and feel that they cannot reveal the very thing that is troubling them so much. One need not soften one's conviction that homosexuality is sinful in order to be compassionate and helpful to a young person with a homosexual problem.

REFER TO QUALIFIED HELP

It is best not to pry into the young person's personal or sex life for details that they have not voluntarily shared with you. Instead, provide information or be a sounding board to help him or her figure out how much of a problem exists. If the problem seems genuine, help the young person find a qualified counselor or professional to talk with. You might even volunteer to accompany the young person to his or her first counseling appointment if that would help.

GIVE WISE ADVICE

Always keep any information you have about the young person's problem in total confidence unless the youth is being exploited illegally (in that case try to get the young person to tell his parents, or approach them yourself). It only makes the problem more difficult to overcome if people know about it and stereotype the young person as a homosexual. The fewer people that know, the better. Instruct the young person, as well, to be careful not to unburden himself about the problem to very many people. Do not let him fall for gay liberation rhetoric about "coming out of the closet"; sexual practices are private and should not be paraded in public, for the young person's own protection as well as for the protection of others who might be adversely affected by such announcements.

Do not ever joke about your friend's homosexual problem to him or to anyone else. Instead, be serious, sober, and mature in discussing the problem when he or she brings it up. In a loving and sensitive manner, help the young person understand the serious ethical and spiritual issues involved.

The person with a problem with homosexual lust or homosexual behavior problems needs divine forgiveness; Christian sympathy and prayer; supportive encouragement for solving the problem from parents and friends; and proper counseling or psychotherapy, or help from an effective Christian ministry to homosexuals.

1. See American Psychological Association, *Removing the Stigma —Final Report of the Board of Social and Ethical Responsibility for Psychology's Task Force on the Status of Lesbian and Gay Male Psychologists* (Washington, D.C.: APA, 1981), for the reports and bibliography endorsed by the American Psychological Association.
2. G. A. Rekers, P. M. Bentler, A. C. Rosen, and O. I. Lovaas, "Child Gender Disturbances: A Clinical Rationale for Intervention," *Psychotherapy: Theory, Research, and Practice* 14 (1977): 2-11; A. C. Rosen, G. A. Rekers, and L. R. Friar, "Theoretical and Diagnostic Issues in Child Gender Disturbances," *Journal of Sex Research* 13 (1977): 89-103; G. A. Rekers, A. C. Rosen, O. I. Lovaas, and P. M. Bentler, "Sex-Role Stereotypy and Professional Intervention for Childhood Gender Disturbances," *Professional Psychology* 9 (1978): 127-36; A. C. Rosen, G. A. Rekers, and P. M. Bentler, "Ethical Issues in the Treatment of Children," *Journal of Social Issues* 34 (1978): 122-36; G. A. Rekers and S. Mead, "Female Sex-Role Deviance: Early Identification and Developmental Intervention," *Journal of Clinical Child Psychology* 9 (1980): 199-203.
3. For a review of psychological treatment studies of adolescents with homosexual problems, see G. A. Rekers, "Sexual Problems: Behavior Modification," in B. B. Wolman, ed., *Handbook of Treatment of Mental Disorders in Childhood and Adolescence* (Englewood Cliffs, N.J.: Prentice-Hall, 1978). For a recent review of the effectiveness of various Christian psychotherapists and Christian outreach ministries to homosexuals, see Tom Minnery, "Homosexuals CAN Change," *Christianity Today* 6 February 1981, pp. 36-41. For a review of studies of psychotherapeutic treatment of adult homosexual problems, see Frank M. duMas, *Gay Is Not Good* (Nashville: Nelson, 1979), chaps. 11-15.
4. G. A. Rekers, "Pathological Sex-Role Development in Boys: Behavioral Treatment and Assessment" (Ph.D. diss., University of California, Los Angeles, 1972); G. A. Rekers, "Assessment and Treatment of Childhood Gender Problems," in B. B. Lahey and A. E. Kazdin, eds., *Advances in Clinical Child Psychology, Vol. 1* (New York: Plenum, 1977); G. A. Rekers and O. I. Lovaas, "Behavioral Treatment of Deviant Sex-Role Behaviors in a Male Child," *Journal of Applied Behavior Analysis* 7 (1974): 173-90;

G. A. Rekers, O. I. Lovaas, and B. P. Low, "The Behavioral Treatment of a 'Transsexual' Preadolescent Boy," *Journal of Abnormal Child Psychology* 2 (1974): 99-116; G. A. Rekers, C. E. Yates, T. J. Willis, A. C. Rosen, and M. Taubman, "Childhood Gender Identity Change: Operant Control over Sex-Typed Play and Mannerisms," *Journal of Behavior Therapy and Experimental Psychiatry* 7 (1976): 51-57; G. A. Rekers and J. W. Varni, "Self-Monitoring and Self-Reinforcement Processes in a Pre-Transsexual Boy," *Behavior Research and Therapy* 15 (1977): 177-80; G. A. Rekers and J. W. Varni, "Self-Regulation of Gender-Role Behaviors: A Case Study," *Journal of Behavior Therapy and Experimental Psychiatry* 8 (1977): 427-32; G. A. Rekers, T. J. Willis, C. E. Yates, A. C. Rosen, and B. P. Low, "Assessment of Childhood Gender Behavior Change," *Journal of Child Psychology and Psychiatry* 18 (1977): 53-65; G. A. Rekers and G. C. Milner, "Sexual Identity Disorders in Childhood and Adolescence," *Journal of the Florida Medical Association* 65 (1978): 962-64; G. A. Rekers, B. F. Crandall, A. C. Rosen, and P. M. Bentler, "Genetic and Physical Studies of Male Children with Psychological Gender Disturbances," *Psychological Medicine* 9 (1979): 373-75; G. A. Rekers, "Childhood Sexual Identity Disorder," *Medical Aspects of Human Sexuality* 15 (1981): 141-42; G. A. Rekers, "Sex-Role Behavior Change: Intrasubject Studies of Boyhood Gender Disturbance," *Journal of Psychology* 103 (1979): 255-69.
5. See Minnery; also duMas.
6. E. Mansell Pattison and Myrna Loy Pattison, "Ex-Gays: Religiously Mediated Change in Homosexuals," *American Journal of Psychiatry* 137 (1980): 1552-62.
7. See G. A. Rekers, "Sexual Problems: Behavior Modification," in B. B. Wolman, ed., *Handbook of Treatment of Mental Disorders in Childhood and Adolescence* for more information on these procedures.

9

"Such Were Some of You"—True Liberation for Homosexuals

The young medical student looked sadly to the ground. "I've been fighting these feelings since I was nine."

His voice was neither defiant nor repentant. Was it resigned?

"It's no use. I am what I am."

I had known Bob for many years. He had taken an active role in our church fellowship and had on many occasions stood before the entire church to speak from God's Word.

It was on one such occasion, when Bob had spoken on a verse of Scripture to the congregation, that everything changed.

In the congregation that morning was another young man—a recent convert. For twelve years he had been "married" to a man and had been deeply enmeshed in the homosexual community. He recognized Bob. Shortly after that meeting, the converted homosexual had lunch with me.

"You know," he said naively, "there are more gays around than you would realize."

"I guess so." I really wasn't listening, but what followed got my full attention.

"Yeah, even one of your own church members is gay." He told me about Bob.

A few minutes later I had arranged a meeting with Bob. His response, recounted above, ended in a hopeless admission of periodic, frustrated efforts to resist temptation followed by "inevitable" failures. He had read all the books, listened to all the rhetoric, and finally decided that homosexuality was neither sinful nor harmful. He wasn't about to surrender the pleasures of his life. He walked out my door, and although we had been friends for nearly eight years, I never saw him again.

What happened was tragic. Bob had fallen victim to the propaganda of the enemy. He became one of the casualties of the sexual revolt. There was help, there was the possibility of change, but Bob would not believe it.

Biblical evidence gives the promise of change.

STARTING OVER

In the Old Testament account of the institution of the Passover, we read, "This month shall be the beginning of months for you; it is to be the first month of the year to you" (Exodus 12:2). At first glance this appears to be a matter-of-fact couplet. Its significance, however, runs deep. The implication of this simple verse is that when God works redemption in His people's lives, He starts them all over again. From that point on, everything is new. The day of Israel's deliverance from Egyptian bondage was the first day of a new life with God. No longer slaves, no longer oppressed, as new people they began a new relationship with the God who makes things new.

"Christ our Passover also has been sacrificed. Let us

therefore celebrate the feast, not with old leaven, nor with the leaven of malice and wickedness, but with the unleavened bread of sincerity and truth" (1 Corinthians 5:7-8). The newness of redemption continues because of what Jesus has done on the cross. Indeed the Passover was only a symbol of an even greater act of redemption and atonement. "Take," Jesus said at His final Passover meal, "eat." At that last supper Jesus showed the disciples an even greater truth. Handling the unleavened bread He said, "This is My body, broken for you." Here is redemption and forgiveness. Here is the basis for starting over.

One of the most familiar texts in the New Testament is 2 Corinthians 5:17: "Therefore if any man is in Christ, he is a new creature; the old things passed away; behold, new things have come." This truth is buttressed by Jesus' own words: "Behold, I am making all things new" (Revelation 21:5). To understand this newness, we have to better understand the dynamic of becoming a Christian.

When someone confesses or agrees with God's judgment on sin, repents of his sin, and calls upon Jesus Christ to be his Savior and Lord, Jesus actually enters that person's life. We often tell our children that Jesus comes into our "hearts." In Ephesians 3:17, Paul prays "that Christ may dwell in your hearts through faith."

But what does that mean? After all, Jesus has a very real body that the Bible says God raised from the dead. When last seen, Jesus ascended into heaven in that very body and the Bible says He is now seated at the right hand of the Father. How can this Jesus live in us? The Bible teaches that when someone becomes a Christian by placing faith in Christ, the Holy Spirit indwells that believer with the very personality of Jesus. Jesus promised us this:

If you love Me, you will keep My commandments. And I will ask the Father, and He will give you another Helper, that He may be with you forever; that is, even the Spirit of truth, whom the world cannot receive, because it does not behold Him or know Him, but you know Him because He abides with you, *and will be in you.* I will not leave you as orphans; I will come to you [John 14:15-18, italics added].

INFINITE POTENTIAL

When someone puts his faith in Christ, that person is given a new life. His old life was under the power of sin and destined for disaster, he was open prey to Satan, and as far as God was concerned he was as good as dead. Listen to Paul's description:

And you were dead in your trespasses and sin, in which you formerly walked according to the course of this world, according to the prince of the power of the air, of the spirit that is now working in the sons of disobedience.

That is to say, the devil is strongly influencing the non-Christian.

Among them we too all formerly lived in the lusts of our flesh, indulging the desires of the flesh and of the mind, and were by nature children of wrath, even as the rest. But God, being rich in mercy, because of His great love with which He loved us, even when we were dead in our transgressions, made us alive together with Christ (by grace you have been saved), and raised us up with Him, and seated us with Him in the heavenly places, in Christ Jesus, in order that in the ages to come He might show the surpassing riches of His grace in kindness toward us in Christ Jesus. For by grace you have been saved through faith; and that not of yourselves, it is the gift of God; not as a result of works, that no one should boast. For we are His workmanship, created in Christ Jesus for good works, which God prepared beforehand, that we should walk in them [Ephesians 2:1-10].

A Christian, no matter how great the problems facing him, has infinite resources at his disposal; he has been "created in Christ Jesus for good works." Paul was so confident of this resource in our lives that he concluded that God "is able to do exceeding abundantly beyond all that we ask or think, according to the power that works within us" (Ephesians 3:20).

Certainly we still have problems. Our bodies and minds have been programmed by the "lusts of our flesh." Such appetites are strong behavioral conditioners, and even though new life may possess us, a struggle ensues. But as we spend time in contact with the Lord, He works at the lifelong process of making us holy. When we become Christians, God does not expect us instantly to become sinless; but His purpose is certainly that we should sin less.

Is this a digression from our discussion of homosexuality? No, not at all. Homosexuality is a very powerful evil force in the lives of men and women who have fallen victims to it. But the dynamics of salvation are such that the power of homosexuality can and must be broken by Jesus Christ. It is not an easy struggle, nor is it the same for everyone. The power of this perversion varies in the lives of people in proportion to the extent of its conditioning of the personality. Nonetheless, the power of Christ is infinitely greater. There is deliverance and there is restoration. The struggle may be long and hard, and all the gifts of the Holy Spirit may have to be brought to bear upon that struggle. There will be victories and defeats in the life of a homosexual who turns to Jesus Christ, but the Bible promises ultimate victory. "Therefore if any man is in Christ, he is a new creature."

But may a person become a Christian and yet continue his homosexual practices if he likes? It is imperative that we know God's mind on the matter and accept

His view, regardless of the world's propaganda. The fact is, God's Word soundly condemns homosexual behavior: "You shall not lie with a male as one lies with a female; it is an abomination" (Leviticus 18:22). Ancient Israel, entrusted with the Word of God and destined to bring forth the Messiah in the midst of a corrupt, pagan world, considered sexual purity to be a matter of national self-interest. Consequently the highest penalty was dealt to the homosexual: "If there is a man who lies with a male as those who lie with a woman, both of them have committed a detestable act; they shall surely be put to death. Their bloodguiltiness is upon them" (Leviticus 20:13).

Although no one should see this as grounds for making homosexuality a capital offense (the Levitical judgments fit into God's purpose for the uniqueness of Israel), we do see in the severity of God's judgment the seriousness of the offense. The whole of Scripture emphasizes God's condemnation of homosexual practices (see, e.g., Genesis 13:13; 19:1-28; Deuteronomy 23:18; Judges 19:22; Isaiah 3:9; Jeremiah 23:14; Matthew 10:15; 11:23-24; 2 Peter 2:6-10; Jude 7).

In 1 Corinthians 6 we read: "Do you not know that the unrighteous shall not inherit the kingdom of God? Do not be deceived; neither fornicators, nor idolators, nor adulterers, nor effeminate, nor homosexuals, nor thieves, nor the covetous, nor drunkards, nor revilers, nor swindlers, shall inherit the kingdom of God" (vv. 9-10).

Similarly, 1 Timothy 1:8-11 teaches us:

Now we know that the Law is good, if one uses it lawfully, realizing the fact that law is not made for a righteous man but for those who are lawless and rebellious, for the ungodly and sinners, for the unholy and profane, for those who kill their fathers or mothers, for murderers and immoral men and homosexuals and kidnappers and liars and perjurers and whatever else is contrary to sound teaching according to the glorious gospel of the blessed God, with which I have been entrusted.

It is interesting to note that Scripture says nothing about "latent homosexuality." Since the Bible was written before such psychological subtleties were identified, such concepts would have been foreign to its first readers. However, improper sexual urges, heterosexual or homosexual, must certainly be seen as wrong (Matthew 5:28; Job 29). The Spirit, if not the explicit teaching of Scripture, urges repentance and a willingness to bring all improper thoughts under the control of the Lord Jesus. Martin Luther rightly compared sinful thoughts to the birds that fly over our heads: they may momentarily distract us, and we cannot stop their unauthorized flights, but we can certainly keep them from building nests in our hair.

The Bible's great concern is with overt homosexual behavior. God says it is wrong and commands us not to indulge in it. That must be understood. But we must also understand that God never commands us to obey Him without also giving us the ability to obey. "No temptation has overtaken you but such as is common to man; and God is faithful, who will not allow you to be tempted beyond what you are able, but with the temptation will provide the way of escape also, that you may be able to endure it" (1 Corinthians 10:13).

THE DANGERS OF HOMOSEXUALITY

All too often Christians merely expound the scriptural indictments against homosexuality without attention to the biblical warnings of its dangers. Two great dangers of homosexuality are noted in Romans 1:24-28:

Therefore God gave them over in the lusts of their hearts to impurity, that their bodies might be dishonored among

137

them. For they exchanged the truth of God for a lie, and worshiped and served the creature rather than the Creator, who is blessed forever. Amen. For this reason God gave them over to degrading passions; for their women exchanged the natural function for that which is unnatural, and in the same way also the men abandoned the natural function of the woman and burned in their desire toward one another, men with men committing indecent acts and receiving in their own persons the due penalty of their error. And just as they did not see fit to acknowledge God any longer, God gave them over to a depraved mind, to do those things which are not proper.

There is, if you will, the danger of a psycho-physiological kickback. As one indulges in homosexuality, God warns, he receives in his own person the due penalty of his error. The Bible teaches that there is physical as well as psychological deterioration in the man or woman who violates the sexual boundaries God has set up. Homosexuality will destroy the whole person. Paul warns, "Flee immorality [a broad term for sexual sin]. Every other sin that a man commits is outside the body, but the immoral man sins against his own body" (1 Corinthians 6:18). Anyone sensitive to this teaching needs desperately to call out to God for deliverance from such a life-threatening evil as homosexuality.

The second danger noted in Romans 1:24-28 is the danger of losing the ability to recognize and receive God's truth. A man's body not only reflects a physical reality; it reflects a spiritual reality as well. We were created, male and female, in the "image of God." Our sexuality is a source of natural revelation concerning the nature and demands of God (Romans 1:19-20). When we indulge in homosexuality we have "exchanged the truth of God for a lie." That is a result not only of the idolatry indicated in Romans 1 but also of dishonoring their bodies. Losing truth about God, or the ability to accept knowledge of God, leaves a man "without excuse" (v. 20) and justly condemned before God. Whoever indulges in homosexuality is given over purposefully by God to even greater sin.

Many homosexual young men and women that I have counseled were disgusted with their lives, but because of shame, habit, fear, and insecurity, they refused to break with the very thing they hated. Perhaps the warnings of Scripture will motivate when nothing else will. Young people must flee from the life-destroying trap of homosexuality, and God promises to be the refuge of anyone who really wants out of the closet. But they must take a step toward Him by accepting His judgment on homosexuality and by obeying Him. Remember, He never commands us to obey Him without giving us the ability to obey Him as well.

A PERFECT PLAN

God's plan for obedience has several steps. The first is conversion. Without Christ in us we can never please the Father. Second, God expects His people to begin a lifelong pattern of sharing thoughts with Him. Daily reflection on His Word is crucial, and continued prayer is essential to enjoying His provisions for us. "If you abide in My word," Jesus told the Jews who believed in him, "you are truly disciples of Mine" (John 8:31). Simply and straightforwardly the psalmist wrote: "How shall a young man keep his way pure? By keeping it according to [God's] word" (Psalm 119:9). "Pray without ceasing," said the apostle Paul (1 Thessalonians 5:17).

God's Word is a plumb line against which we can constantly judge our own lives and adjust them accordingly. In prayer we can confess our sins to obtain forgiveness (1 John 1:9; 5:13-14) and we can reinforce our intentions to follow Him. Through the reading of

Scripture and prayer, we can be filled with the Holy Spirit. As we pray and respond obediently to God's commands, we experience His promises of the fullness of the Spirit.

There is therefore now no condemnation for those who are in Christ Jesus. For the law of the Spirit of life in Christ Jesus has set you free from the law of sin and of death. For what the Law could not do, weak as it was through the flesh, God did: sending His own Son in the likeness of sinful flesh and as an offering for sin, He condemned sin in the flesh, in order that the requirement of the Law might be fulfilled in us, who do not walk according to the flesh, but according to the Spirit [Romans 8:1-4].

Christians must walk "according to the Spirit," not "according to the flesh." When one becomes a Christian, whatever his difficulties, he always has the choice of following either Christ or the dictates of his own sin-permeated body and mind. The more time he spends under God's influence, in obedient response to His Word and in prayer, the better able he is to choose to "walk according to the Spirit."

Following conversion and a decision to begin a life of sharing thoughts with God, the third step is to be full of the Holy Spirit. What does this mean? It means that we must face up to sin and constantly confess sin to God, since sin offends God's Spirit (Ephesians 4:30). However, we must remember that a thorough knowledge of our sin is impossible. The psalmist recognized this and prayed, "Who can discern his errors? Acquit me of hidden faults" (Psalm 19:12). A contrite heart takes into account that there is sin in its life to which it is insensitive, and asks forgiveness for this as well.

Although I dislike pat formulas for being filled with the Holy Spirit, I do recognize that the biblical pattern contains the elements of prayer, longing for power to serve God, and involvement with other Christians.

Therefore be careful how you walk, not as unwise men, but as wise, making the most of your time, because the days are evil. So then do not be foolish, but understand what the will of the Lord is. And do not get drunk with wine, for that is dissipation, but be filled with the Spirit, speaking to one another in psalms and hymns and spiritual songs, singing and making melody with your heart to the Lord; always giving thanks for all things in the name of our Lord Jesus Christ to God, even the Father [Ephesians 5:15-20].

This brings us to the fourth and final step, which is participation in Christian fellowship. Interaction with other Christians is crucial to growth and healthy Christian living. God has designed us to respond to Him best in a company of likeminded people. We need their support, their unique abilities, and the direction God may give as individuals. Whatever struggles we face in life are intended by God to be lessened by being divided. "Bear one another's burdens, and thus fulfill the law of Christ" (Galatians 6:2).

As with anyone else, so it is with the homosexual who turns to Christ. God will deliver him as he accepts God's judgment upon his homosexuality, as he comes to Christ for salvation, as he prayerfully and obediently responds to God's Word, as he earnestly seeks to be filled with the Holy Spirit, and as he shares his life with others who have made a similar commitment to Christ. However intense his struggle, however deeply affected his personality, the homosexual who accepts God's method will know victory over his or her sexual problem.

WHAT ABOUT THE CHURCH?

There is another dimension to the problem of homosexuality today: the intolerance of many believers toward the homosexual. Sadly, many Christians place a special onus on those who have fallen into sexual sin. When the apostle Paul condemned the act of homosexuality, in the same breath he condemned adultery, thievery, greed, drunkenness, and other sins (1 Corinthians 6:9-10). But he noted with joy that even though many Christians had had those problems, they had also found forgiveness, holiness, and cleansing in their new walk with Christ. "And *such were some of you;* but you were washed . . . sanctified . . . justified in the name of the Lord Jesus Christ, and in the Spirit of our God" (1 Corinthians 6:11, italics added). Would to God more Christians would follow Paul's example.

The church of Jesus Christ, while keeping high standards of holiness, should always show the love and acceptance that her Lord showed to the sinner. Many homosexuals that I have encountered are desperately unhappy, and many are afraid. One often gets the impression that if only they could find a supportive community, they would certainly attempt to turn their backs on the perversion that binds them. How sad that the church, which should be that kind of a community, often earns the reputation for being precisely the opposite.

In its concern for the lost, the church should seek out the homosexual. In its varied expressions of love, the church should welcome the homosexual. The true contagion of homosexuality is not in the homosexual himself but in the will that openly rebels against God. Our homophobia should be biblical; we should not fear the homosexual, but we should fear his sin.

A TWO-WAY STREET

A word should be said about the homosexual seeking to overcome his problem. Intolerance should never drive him away from people the Lord wants him to love. We are all sinners. Intolerance is never conquered

142

by intolerance. Many in the church today react the way they do because they are afraid and angered by the rhetoric of the gay liberation movement. Their fear is valid even if their intolerance is not. But remember, Jesus did not leave us an option regarding the church. We are to be wholeheartedly committed to the church. We can't indulge in smugness at the expense of God's people. Catching them in the sin of intolerance is not a license for the homosexual to shoot back.

Forgiveness and understanding must start somewhere. In truth, the first steps toward a forgiving New Testament community are in the heart of each individual.

Suggested Reading

BOOKS

Braun, M., and Rekers, G. A. *The Christian in an Age of Sexual Eclipse*. Wheaton, Ill.: Tyndale, 1981.

Court, John H. *Pornography: A Christian Critique*. Downers Grove, Ill.: Inter-Varsity, 1980.

Davidson, Alex. *The Returns of Love: A Contemporary Christian View of Homosexuality*. Downers Grove, Ill.: Inter-Varsity, 1970.

Dillow, Joseph C. *Solomon on Sex*. New York: Nelson, 1977.

duMas, Frank M. *Gay Is Not Good*. Nashville: Nelson, 1979.

Enroth, Ronald M., and Jamison, Gerald E. *The Gay Church*. Grand Rapids: Eerdmans, 1974.

Field, David. *The Homosexual Way—A Christian Option?* Rev. ed. Downers Grove, Ill.: Inter-Varsity, 1979.

LaHaye, Tim. *The Unhappy Gays: What Everyone Should Know About Homosexuality*. Wheaton, Ill.: Tyndale, 1978.

Miles, Herbert J. *Sexual Happiness in Marriage*. Grand Rapids: Zondervan, 1967.

———. *Sexual Understanding Before Marriage*. Grand Rapids: Zondervan, 1971.

Payne, Leanne. *The Broken Image*. Westchester, Ill.: Cornerstone, 1981.

Rekers, G. A. "Assessment and Treatment of Childhood Gender Problems." In *Advances in Clinical Child Psychology*, Vol. 1, edited by B. B. Lahey and A. E. Kazdin. New York: Plenum, 1977.

————. "Play Therapy with Cross-Gender Identified Boys." In *Handbook of Play Therapy*, edited by Charles E. Schaefer and Kevin J. O'Connor. New York: John Wiley, 1982.

————. "Psychosexual and Gender Problems." In *Behavioral Assessment of Childhood Disorders*, edited by E. J. Mash and L. G. Terdal. New York: Guilford, 1981.

————. "Sexual Problems: Behavior Modification." In *Handbook of Treatment of Mental Disorders in Childhood and Adolescence*, edited by B. B. Wolman. Englewood Cliffs, N.J.: Prentice-Hall, 1978.

————. *Shaping Your Child's Sexual Identity*. Grand Rapids: Baker, 1982.

————. "Therapies Dealing with the Child's Sexual Difficulties." In *Enfance et Sexualite/Childhood and Sexuality*, edited by Jean-Marc Samson. Montreal and Paris: Les Editions Etudes Vivantes, 1980.

Rekers, G. A., and Jurich, A. P. "Development of Problems of Puberty and Sex Roles in Adolescents." In *Handbook of Clinical Psychology*, edited by C. Eugene Walker and Michael C. Roberts. New York: John Wiley, 1982.

Schaeffer, Francis A. *True Spirituality*. Wheaton, Ill.: Tyndale, 1971.

Wheat, Ed, and Wheat, Gaye. *Intended for Pleasure*. Rev. ed. Old Tappan, N.J.: Revell, 1981.

JOURNALS

Bentler, P. M.; Rekers, G. A.; and Rosen, A. C. "Congruence of Childhood Sex-Role Identity and Behavior Disturbances." *Child: Care, Health, and Development* 5 (1979): 267-84.

Ferguson, L. N., and Rekers, G. A. "Non-Aversive Intervention for Public Childhood Masturbation." *The Journal of Sex Research* 15, 3 (1979): 213-23. Reprinted (digested) in Howard Millman, Jeffrey Cohen, and Charles Schaefer, eds., *Therapies for School Behavior Problems* (San Francisco: Jossey-Bass, 1980).

Minnery, Tom. "Homosexuals CAN Change." *Christianity Today*, 6 February 1981, pp. 36-41.

Pattison, E. Mansell, and Pattison, Myrna Loy. "Ex-Gays: Religiously Mediated Change in Homosexuals." *American Journal of Psychiatry* 137, 12 (December 1980): 1553-62.

Rekers, G. A. "A Priori Values and Research on Homosexuality." *American Psychologist* 33 (1978): 510-12.

————. "Atypical Gender Development and Psychosocial Adjustment." *Journal of Applied Behavior Analysis* 10 (1977): 559-71.

————. "Childhood Sexual Identity Disorders." *Medical Aspects of Human Sexuality* 15, 3 (1981): 141-42.

————. "Sex-Role Behavior Change: Intrasubject Studies of Boyhood Gender Disturbance." *The Journal of Psychology* 103 (1979): 255-69.

————. "Stimulus Control over Sex-Typed Play in Cross-Gender Identified Boys." *Journal of Experimental Child Psychology* 20 (1975): 136-48.

Rekers, G. A.; Amaro-Plotkin, H.; and Low, B. P. "Sex-Typed Mannerisms in Normal Boys and Girls as a Function of Sex and Age." *Child Development* 48 (1977): 275-78.

Rekers, G. A.; Bentler, P. M.; Rosen, A. C.; and Lovaas, O. I. "Child Gender Disturbances: A Clinical Rationale for Intervention." *Psychotherapy: Theory, Research, and Practice* 14 (1977): 2-11.

Rekers, G. A.; Crandall, B. F.; Rosen, A. C.; and Bentler, P. M. "Genetic and Physical Studies of Male Children with Psychological Gender Disturbances." *Psychological Medicine* 9 (1979): 373-75.

Rekers, G. A., and Lovaas, O. I. "Behavioral Treatment of Deviant Sex-Role Behaviors in a Male Child." *Journal of Applied Behavior Analysis* 7 (1974): 173-90. Reprinted as chapter 25 in C. M. Franks and G. T. Wilson, eds., *Annual Review of Behavior Therapy and Practice* (New York: Brunner/Mazel, 1975). Reprinted as chapter 38 in G. R. Patterson, I. M. Marks, J. D. Mazarazzo, R. A. Myers, G. E. Schwartz, and H. H. Strupp, eds., *Behavior Change 1974: An Aldine Annual on Psychotherapy, Counseling, and Behavior Modification* (Chicago: Aldine, 1975).

Rekers, G. A., and Lovaas, O. I. "Experimental Analysis of Cross-Sex Behavior in Male Children." *Research Relating to Children* 28 (1971): 68.

Rekers, G. A.; Lovaas, O. I.; and Low, B. P. "The Behavioral Treatment of a 'Transsexual' Preadolescent Boy." *Journal of Abnormal Child Psychology* 2 (1974): 99-116. Reprinted (digested) in Howard L. Millman, Jeffrey J. Cohen, and Charles E. Schaefer, eds., *Therapies for School Behavior Problems* (San Francisco: Jossey-Bass, 1980), pp. 305-7.

Rekers, G. A., and Mead, S. "Early Intervention for Female Sexual Identity Disturbance: Self-Monitoring of Play Behavior." *Journal of Abnormal Child Psychology* 7, 4 (1979): 405-23.

———. "Female Sex-Role Deviance: Early Identification and Developmental Intervention." *Journal of Clinical Child Psychology* 9, 3 (1980): 199-203. Cited in "Development of Social Skills," *University of Sheffield Biomedical Information Service* 1, 3 (March 1981):4.

———. "Human Sex Differences in Carrying Behaviors: A Replication and Extension." *Perceptual and Motor Skills* 48 (1979): 625-26.

Rekers, G. A.; Mead, S. L.; Rosen, A. C.; and Brigham, S. L. "Family Correlates of Male Childhood Gender Disturbance." *The Journal of Genetic Psychology*, in press.

Rekers, G. A., and Milner, G. C. "Early Detection of Sexual Identity Disorders." *Medical Aspects of Human Sexuality* 15, 11 (1981): 32EE-32FF.

———. "How to Diagnose and Manage Childhood Sexual Disorders." *Behavioral Medicine* 6, 4 (1979): 18-21.

———. "Sexual Identity Disorders in Childhood and Adolescence." *Journal of the Florida Medical Association* 65 (1978): 926-64.

Rekers, G. A.; Rosen, A. C.; Lovaas, O. I.; and Bentler, P. M. "Sex-Role Stereotypy and Professional Intervention for Childhood Gender Disturbances," *Professional Psychology* 9 (1978): 127-36.

Rekers, G. A., and Rudy, J. P. "Differentiation of Childhood Body Gestures," *Perceptual and Motor Skills* 46 (1978): 839-45.

Rekers, G. A.; Sanders, J. A.; and Strauss, C. C. "Developmental Differentiation of Adolescent Body Gestures." *Journal of Genetic Psychology* 138, 1 (1981): 123-31.

Rekers, G. A.; Sanders, J. A.; Strauss, C. C.; Rasbury, W. C.; and Mead, S. L. "Differentiation of Adolescent Activity Participation." *The Journal of Genetic Psychology*, in press.

Rekers, G. A., and Varni, J. W. "Self-Monitoring and Self-Reinforcement Processes in a Pre-Transsexual Boy." *Behavior Research and Therapy* 15 (1977): 177-80.

———. "Self-Regulation of Gender-Role Behaviors: A Case Study." *Journal of Behavior Therapy and Experimental Psychiatry* 8 (1977): 427-32.

Rekers, G. A.; Willis, T. J.; Yates, C. E.; Rosen, A. C.; and Low, B. P. "Assessment of Childhood Gender Behavior Change." *Journal of Child Psychology and Psychiatry* 18 (1977): 53-65.

Rekers, G. A., and Yates, C. E. "Sex-Typed Play in Feminoid Boys vs. Normal Boys and Girls." *Journal of Abnormal Child Psychology*, 4 (1976): 1-8.

Rekers, G. A.; Yates, C. E.; Willis, T. J.; Rosen, A. C.; and Taubman, M. "Childhood Gender Identity Change: Operant Control over Sex-Typed Play and Mannerisms." *Journal of Behavior Therapy and Experimental Psychiatry*, 7 (1976): 51-57.

Rosen, A. C.; Rekers, G. A.; and Friar, L. R. "Theoretical and Diagnostic Issues in Child Gender Disturbances." *The Journal of Sex Research* 13, 2 (1977): 89-103.

Rosen, A. C.; Rekers, G. A.; and Bentler, P. M. "Ethical Issues in the Treatment of Children." *Journal of Social Issues*, 34, 2 (1978): 122-36. Reprinted in *Eta Evolutiva*, 1979 (an Italian scientific review).

Rosen, A. C., and Rekers, G. A. "Toward a Taxonomic Framework for Variables of Sex and Gender." *Genetic Psychology Monographs*, 102 (1980): 191-218.

Sims, Bennett J. "Sex and Homosexuality." *Christianity Today*, 24 February 1978, pp. 23-30.

Topical Index

151

Gomorrah, 40-41
Gonorrhea, 53. *See also* Venereal disease
Gospel, 31, 122
Guilt, 49, 110, 119-20, 122

H

Harvard University, 9
Hay, Henry, 34
Healing, 31, 124-26
Health, 33, 53, 102, 120, 141
Hebrew, 40
Hell, 41, 101
Hepatitis, 54
Heterosexual, heterosexuality, 15, 20-21, 29-30, 36, 47, 49, 52-54, 64, 66, 68, 70, 73, 78, 81-83, 102, 111, 121, 124, 137. *See also* Marriage
Holy, holiness, 142
Holy Spirit, 133-35, 137, 140-42
Home, 31, 65-66, 73-76. *See also* Family
Homophobia, 14-15, 20-21, 142
Homosexual bar, 35, 99, 103, 105. *See also* "Gay bar"
Homosexual
 behavior, 22-25, 39, 47, 53, 67, 70, 78, 91-96, 102, 117, 120, 122, 129, 136-37
 effeminate, 22, 37, 68
 experimentation, 20
 fantasy, 92, 112, 118, 125. *See also* Homosexual, lust
 fetishistic, 37
 identity, 110. *See also* Sexual, identity
 lust, 23-25, 91-93, 102-3, 112, 117, 119-20, 122, 129
 memories, 91-92
 militants, 33, 35, 45
 murderers, 27
 obsession, 100, 110
 orientation, 50, 93, 95-96, 115, 124

pornography, 37, 91, 93, 103, 105, 117, 125
prostitute, 36, 101-2, 113
rape, 23
revolt, 34, 38
sado-masochistic, 37
sex play, 20
sin, 25, 41, 91
temptation, 15, 24-25, 47, 65, 67, 69, 73-74, 76, 81-83, 87, 91-94, 97, 102-5, 111-12, 117-20, 123
tendencies, 63-65, 69
Homosexuality
 causes of, 63-71
 definition of, 22-23, 64-65
 ego-dystonic, 49
 incestuous, introduced by a parent, 63, 69, 77, 91
 trap of, 25-26, 63-106, 139
 triumph over, 107-27, 132-37
 types, 22
Hope, 95, 109, 127, 132-37
Hormonal, 64-65, 121
Humanistic, humanism, 29-31, 51, 57

I

Image of God, 138
Immorality, 23-25, 39, 89, 138. *See also* Sin
Indecent acts, 138
Institute for Sex Research, 70
Intercourse, 40

J

Jesus Christ, 13-15, 40, 80, 90, 132-35, 137, 139-43
Judeo-Christian, 41, 51, 115. *See also* Christian

L

Law(s), legality, 97, 113
Learning experiences, 75

Legg, Dorr, 34
Lesbian, 34, 50, 52, 88
"Liberation," "liberationist," 48, 64, 69, 80, 82. See also "Gay liberation"
Life-style, 27-28, 32, 39, 53, 82, 96, 100-1. See also "Alternative life-style"
Logos Research Institute, Inc., 10
Loneliness, 49, 100
Lot, 40-41
Lovaas, Dr. O. Ivan, 9
Love, loving, 22, 47, 52, 97, 102, 127, 129, 142
Lust, 25, 89, 91, 97, 105, 117, 135. See also Homosexual, lust

M

"Macho," 37. See also Masculine
Mannerisms, 147
Marriage, 25, 29-31, 47, 52, 54, 70, 73, 77, 79, 82, 88, 97-98, 101-2, 105, 110-11, 116, 120, 125
Masculine, 22, 68, 76. See also "Macho"
Masculinity, 74-75
Masturbation, 24
Mattachine Society, 34
Medical College of Georgia, 122
Mental disorder or disturbance, 23-24, 30, 50, 52. See also Psychological disorder
Mental illness, 23-24, 30, 46, 48-50, 52. See also Emotional disturbance, Psychological, disorder
Meyerhoff Park, 45
Moral
beliefs, 122
choice, 25. See also Choice
consequence, 99, 112
order, 103
standards, 35, 38-39

Mother, motherhood, 29, 67, 70, 74-79, 88-89, 110-11.

N

National Institute of Mental Health, 9
National Science Foundation, 9
Natural, 80-82
Nervous system, 92-94, 102, 124
New York City Health Department, 53
Noah, 41
Norm, 29-30, 48, 51, 54
Nude, 27, 77

O

ONE, Inc., 34

P

Passion(s), 138
Passover, 132-33
Pastoral counselor, 116
Pattison, Dr. Mansell, 122
Permissiveness, 15
Personality, 133, 135, 141
Perversion, 23, 33, 38, 48, 135, 142
Physician, 28, 53
Politics, political, 28, 36, 39, 46, 50-51, 114
Pornography, 37, 91. See also Homosexual, pornography
Prayer, 80, 90, 122, 129, 139-40
Premarital sexual relations, 70
Promiscuity, 22, 53-54, 58, 99-100, 120
Prostitution, 35, 113
Psychiatric social worker, 116
Psychiatrist, 14, 28, 30, 52, 55-56, 82, 114, 116
Psychiatry, 28, 47-48, 54
Psychological
adjustment, 113

Scripture Index